the dinah project

the
dinah
project

*A Handbook for
Congregational
Response to
Sexual Violence*

MONICA A. COLEMAN

THE PILGRIM PRESS

CLEVELAND

The Pilgrim Press, 700 Prospect Avenue, Cleveland, Ohio 44115-1100
thepilgrimpress.com

09   08   07   06   05   04   5   4   3   2   1

Library of Congress Cataloging-in-Publication Data

Coleman, Monica A., 1974–
    The Dinah Project: a handbook for congregational response to sexual violence /
Monica A. Coleman.
        p.   cm.
    Includes bibliographical references.
    SBN 0-8298-1587-2 (pbk. : alk. paper)
        1. Rape victims—Services for—United States.   2. Church and social problems—
United States.   3. Church work—United States.   I. Title.

HV6561.C65   2004
261.8'3272—dc22

                                                    2004046515

dedication

To Dinah—whose words fell out of the tradition, but whose memory we cherish.

To all who have been touched by the experience of sexual violence and long to include God in their process of healing.

To God be the glory.

contents

preface

T he Dinah Project is a very small idea that blossomed into a ministry. It is the result of my refusal to abandon the church in my own process of healing from the trauma of rape. It is the result of the vision of a pastor who understood that this is an important issue to address in our community. Most importantly, it is the result of the numerous named and unnamed persons who supported the ministry in its infancy and as it grew.

In 1996 when I was twenty-one, I was raped. It was almost three years after accepting my call to the ministry and nearly one year into my studies in divinity school. My commitment to both God and the church had just recently transformed from that of an active church member to that of a professional. I was still trying to figure out what that meant. In the middle of this process, I was raped by a man who was also a seminarian, and also clergy. And I didn't have much of anything to say to God.

I had talked to God throughout the rape, pleading for intervention. Pleading that somehow, some way, God would stop this thing from happening to me. After the rape, there was no more pleading and no more praying. Honestly, I was absolutely disgusted that the same God to whom

I prayed and whom I worshipped was the same God to whom my rapist would pray and worship. It was too much for me to handle.

I shared my story very slowly and with apprehension. Although it was months before I used the word, "rape," I managed to tell the people I felt could be of the greatest assistance in facilitating my daily life activities once again. I told the people I had to. I told my employer because I could not manage to get up and go to work. I told my best friend because I could not make it through a day without crying. I told my academic advisor because I did not think I would make it through exams and final term papers. I told the pastor of my church because I could not imagine how I could be a minister to anyone at that time in my life.

My experience with the church was very discouraging. When I told the pastor of the church where I served, he listened to me while watching a sports event on a television above my head. The pastor replied, "I have heard of similar situations happening to other members of the church. But no one ever told me directly; I heard about it other ways." That was the beginning and end of the compassion I received in that location. It was also the last Sunday that I served at that church.

The second pastor in whom I confided offered a response that was only slightly more sympathetic. I sat crying in his office, and he asked me, "Well, what was he [the man who raped you] doing in your apartment anyway?" I forgot anything that he said after that point, but I remember going home and asking myself over and over again how I could have allowed this to happen to me. I was convinced that the rape was my fault.

The third pastor in whom I confided told me that depression was a tool of the enemy and that I should cast it out in the name of Jesus. I cast, and I cast, and I was still an emotional wreck.

Six months after being raped, I was still without a church home; yet I had the academic obligation of finding a place in which to serve as a minister. In order to maintain my proposed plan of study in divinity school, I needed to contract with a church for the duration of one school year. I had visited five churches in the intervening six months and was almost hopeless. Every time I had turned to a trusted associate in ministry, I went home in more pain than I had come with. Each time I went to church for the reassurance that God cared and that there was still a place for me in ministry, I returned with decreasing confidence in my own calling as a minister and the church as an institution for the wounded and broken. If I had not been a minister, if I had not been compelled to find a place for studying ministry, I fear I might have left the church altogether.

[handwritten notes in top margin: Chi response to sexual violence (worship / community / educate / counsel)]

Finally I returned to a small church I had visited a few times with a classmate. In this place, I could cry and no one stared at me. In fact, they hugged and offered tissues. In this place, people openly spoke of the addictions and illnesses they were still trying to overcome and the congregation applauded based on effort alone. After attending a few services, I decided to work at this church.

By this time, I'd had some counseling, I had done some reading, and I had a language for my experience. I sat down with the pastor for the first time and declared, "Look, I was just raped six months ago, and I am posttraumatic. I don't know if I am having a good day or a bad day until I wake up. And then I don't know if I can get out of bed. I don't think I make a very good minister because I need someone to minister to me. Can you work with that?"

With a smile, the pastor replied, "Why don't you just show up and we'll figure out the ministry part later?"

"Later" came in December of 1996. I had continued psychological counseling; I was pursuing legal avenues for justice; and I was reading all I could about the psychological and theological effects of sexual violence. But there was something missing. I still struggled in my personal relationship with God. I didn't quite know how to pray anymore. I didn't know how to worship God anymore. I didn't know if I should be angry with God for being raped, or thankful for surviving the rape. When I tried to explain my confusion to my therapist, she understood, but she had no answers. When I tried to explain to my professors, they offered bibliographic suggestions, but no answers. I knew how to go through the motions of liturgy and preaching, but I wanted to "feel God" again. I wanted to include God in my process of healing.

I decided to create my own ritual. I decided that I wanted to invite friends and family and have a small church ceremony. Maybe the laying-on of hands? Something that involved people I loved, a church tradition, and touching. A healing touch—a touch that would not frighten me.

In December, I asked my pastor if I could use the church for a small ceremony. Rather than saying "yes" or "no," he asked me to pray about it. "I think," he said warmly, "That this may be something a little bigger."

Something bigger became the first Dinah Project worship service on June 1, 1997. With the help of friends, faculty, church staff, and church members, a small committee of individuals fumbled their way through organizing a community worship experience that talked about sexual violence in the church.

After three years, The Dinah Project had taken on a life bigger than me and bigger than the church in which it was founded. With trial, error, and a lot of grace, The Dinah Project organized a church response to sexual violence through worship, community education, and counseling. The Dinah Project has been my own saving grace for the mere fact that it made the difference between a vacuous spiritual life and including God in my healing process. It made the difference between a growing skepticism for churches and clergy, and a belief and understanding that the church *can* be a safe place for those who have experienced sexual violence. The Dinah Project helped me to see beyond my own experience and pains to the larger community that also desires healing, compassion, and safety.

It is my hope that The Dinah Project can do the same for you, your church, and your community. As I share lessons learned and curriculum used, I hope that you have a starting place for your local church and community for being an instrument of the compassionate caring presence of God in the midst of evil and pain.

You may know and love someone who has experienced rape. Perhaps you were looking for the right thing to do and say, and came up speechless. Perhaps you have seen news stories about victims of rape and offered up a quick prayer. Or perhaps you have read some of the scholarly material about the effects of sexual violence. Still, you ask, what now?

So what now? There is no shortage of literature on the effects of sexual violence. A quick library search can yield volumes and volumes of works on the psychological effects and legal nuances of rape, sexual assault, and incest. As a seminary student, I was able to identify the small, but growing, body of literature on the theological and ethical ramifications of sexual violence. What I was not able to find was a how-to book. Once I become steeped in the lingo discussing the traumatic aftereffects that can characterize the experiences of victims, what do I do now? Once I become aware of all the specifically religious issues of sexual violence, what do I do now? Once I am convinced that sexual violence is an issue that the church should address, what do I do now?

This book is about one church's answer to the "what now?" It is about the ministry of an urban church in the southeastern United States. This book is about one interdenominational attempt to give an organized church response to sexual violence. It shares the experiment of a body of believers who dared to say "rape" and "love" from the same pulpit.

Ultimately, this book is for church leaders who want to do something. It is for those who want to talk about sexual violence in their churches.

This book is for people who want to host one program, work with other agencies, or develop entire components within their ministries addressing sexual violence. This book is for you.

I owe an unspeakable debt to The Dinah Project itself. I will always feel love and a sense of safety among Metropolitan Interdenominational Church in Nashville, Tennessee, and the Senior Servant, Rev. Edwin C. Sanders II. I thank Janice Black Moore, my sister in the ministry, who first asked me if I had ever written anything about this ministry and thereby encouraged me to begin this book. I also thank the E. Rhodes and Leona B. Carpenter Foundation and the Carpenter Program in Religion, Gender and Sexuality at Vanderbilt Divinity School for facilitating and supporting my academic study of sexual violence and ministry. I also greatly appreciate my editor Kim Sadler and The Pilgrim Press for their belief in the success of this project.

Special thanks to Tanya Marcovna Barnett, who sat with me during the worst times, and Mai and David Duff, whose love and hospitality enabled me to rest and heal. Without these midwives to my own healing, there would be no Dinah Project.

I thank all the people who played a big role in The Dinah Project: Tim Tohill and Char Creson at the Rape and Sexual Abuse Center of Middle Tennessee; the ministers who gave their time and talent to Dinah Project worship services—Angela Edwards, Martin Espinosa, Linda Hollies, Meriann Taylor, and Frank Thomas; the ministerial staff at Metropolitan Interdenominational Church—David Cassidy, Christopher Davis, Eric Lee, Joanne Robertson, Terry Terrell, and Neely Williams; the Voices of Metropolitan, who were always ready at a moment's notice; Cynithea Reeder for her amazing graphic art. A special vat of gratitude goes to Cynthia Turner-Graham, Leah Fennell, and David Smith for their any-time-all-the-time support of me and Dinah. Thank you, Connie Tuttle and Circle of Grace Community Church, for good theological conversation and for lots of love while working on the manuscript. Special thanks to Eric Jerome Dickey for meeting me for coffee and being the nonreligion person to read the early versions of the manuscript. And thanks to Avis Littleton, whose entry into my life reminded me of Dinah's power and importance and inspired me to "be a minister again" and finish this script. I thank Professor Renita Weems, who made sure I did not fall through the cracks of life, but went above and beyond the call of duty in supporting both The Dinah Project and me. Special thanks to my mother, Pauline A. Bigby, for constantly celebrating my commitment and passion for Dinah. To all the Dinah Project volunteers and clients, I salute you.

1

invocation

- One in six women are victims of rape or attempted rape.
- A total of 17.7 million women have been victims of sexual assault or rape.
- One in ten rape victims is a male.
- Almost half of all rape victims are under age eighteen.
- Three in twenty rape victims are under age twelve.
- Ninety-three percent of juvenile sexual assault victims knew their attacker.
- Eighty percent of rape victims are under age thirty.
- Approximately 95 percent of rape victims knew, loved, or trusted their assailant prior to the attack.
- In 2001, 249,000 people were the victims of rape, attempted rape, or sexual assault.

- Rape is the most under-reported violent crime, with only one in three victims reporting.

- The most common reasons given by victims for not reporting these crimes are: the belief that it is a private or personal matter, and that they fear reprisal from the assailant.

- For years following a rape, 60 percent of rape victims experience post-traumatic stress disorder and 16 percent still suffer with emotional problems fifteen years following the rape.

- Factoring in unreported rapes, fifteen out of sixteen rapists will never spend a day in jail.

- An overwhelming majority of rape service agencies believe that public education about rape, and expanded counseling and advocacy services for the rape victim, would be effective in increasing the willingness of victims to report rapes to the police.

These numbers are people with lives.[1] These numbers are people with hopes and dreams, joys and possibilities, despairs and frustrations, terrors and nightmares. These numbers are people with mothers and fathers, friends and lovers, sons and daughters. These numbers are children and elderly, young adults and the middle-aged. These numbers are people and places all around us. These numbers are the children of God.

Amen.

2

the church's problem

Rape. Sexual assault. Molestation. Attempted rape. Date rape. Incest. Sexual abuse. Sexual violence. These are words usually spoken in whispered tones. These are words we don't like to say out loud. These are words that make us shake our heads and lower our voices and be quiet. Because we don't like to think about it. We don't like to put a picture to it. We don't want to see the pain and ugliness that we know accompanies experiences of sexual violence. And so, we say nothing.

The silence is misleading. When we think of violent crimes, we think of homicides and muggings. News reports of rapes are infrequent enough to stand out in our minds. Few people openly discuss their experiences of rape or sexual assault at work or in casual conversation. We really don't hear about it very much. Although the silence may indicate a lack of a problem, the statistics scream loudly in our ears. One in six women, one in twelve boys, one in six children. These numbers remind us that sexual violence is all around us. It is in our homes, our families, our schools, our workplaces, and our churches.

Sexual violence is the most underreported violent crime in America today, and yet even the most socially active churches fail to address the crisis of sexual violence.[1] Perhaps it is a fear of discussing any issue pertaining to sexuality. Perhaps pastors, clergy, and congregations feel ill equipped to address this crisis. Perhaps churches feel as though it is not their place to address this issue. Perhaps churches believe that their silence on this issue is harmless. Whatever the reason, the church *must* respond.

Every congregation contains victims of sexual violence. Every church with women, men, boys, girls, or the elderly contains victims of sexual violence. Whether an individual confides in the church leaders, family, or friends, or chooses to remain silent, there is no church void of the people whose lives are changed by experiences of sexual violence. Because every church contains persons affected by sexual violence, the church must respond. Because sexual violence affects every aspect of our communities, including our religious and spiritual lives, the church must respond. Because silence is a response of tolerance, the church must respond.

Currently there is little church response to sexual violence. One reason for this silence is a misperception of sexual violence. Sexual violence is often perceived as a female problem. Many people believe sexual violence is a crime that only victimizes women. The term "sexual violence" tends to conjure images of the woman who is raped in a parking lot by a stranger.

One reason for the church's silence is that sexual violence is often considered a social ill. Law enforcement officials must respond to sexual violence as a crime. Medical personnel are equipped to respond to rape as a crime involving physical injuries. Even as we recognize the emotional effects of sexual violence, it is left to the psychological community to address these issues. Sexual violence is seen as a crime that rips into the fabric of the *social* order. The church may have a false understanding of sexual violence as a female social problem that some other agency will address.

We need the church. There is a need for an explicitly religious response to this crisis of sexual violence. First, there is a large amount of biblical ambiguity about sexual violence. The story of Sodom and Gomorrah does not condemn the attempted gang rape of Lot's visitors. The story of Dinah's rape involves vengeance, but it does not mention Dinah outside the fact of her rape. The story of Tamar's incestuous rape encourages Tamar's silence. Some Levitical rules condemn rape; others do not. The story of Potiphar's wife and Joseph leads many people to believe that women often lie about being raped. The second chapter of Revelation justifies the rape of Jezebel as punishment for her false prophecy. Some biblical passages seem to support the unconditional submission of children to parents regardless of abuse. The list continues. If one looks for a single unified biblical response to sexual violence, it cannot be found. These passages need attention and interpretation in the context of the pervasive extent of sexual violence.

Second, there are numerous religious and spiritual effects of sexual violence. Many victims of sexual violence question God's presence and agency as they deal with extreme suffering in the context of their faith. For the Christian victim of sexual violence, concepts of forgiveness and evil arise in new ways and must be addressed. Although there are legal, medical, and psychological personnel to respond to many aspects of sexual violence, only the religious institutions are trained, equipped, and permitted to address issues from a spiritual perspective. Only the church can speak to the presence of God in the midst of the experience of sexual violence. Only the church can bring words of hope, promise, and healing in a society torn by the evil of sexual violence. Only the church can speak of God's unconditional love, unfailing grace, and power to restore the fallen and heal the broken.

Third, there is a need for a compassionate response to sexual violence in our midst. For every incident of sexual violence, there are the victims, the victimizers, and the people who love both or either of them. They all go into some state of crisis. They are all traumatized. We may find that these parties exist within the same family and within the same church. Do we embrace? Do we ignore? Do we judge and condemn? The church is called to give the kind of response that legal, psychological, and medical personnel do not and cannot give. The church is called to name and condemn sin where it is found, but also to extend God's love and grace to all human beings. To be able to find righteous indignation, justice, grace, and love in a situation of horror and violence is nothing but the work of God.

3

(handwritten notes in margin: "1) Jacob - wasted Shechem 2)")

dinah's project

Now Dinah the daughter of Leah, whom she had borne to Jacob, went out to visit the women of the region. When Shechem son of Hamor the Hivite, prince of the region, saw her, he seized her and lay with her by force. And his soul was drawn to Dinah daughter of Jacob; he loved the girl, and spoke tenderly to her. So Shechem spoke to his father Hamor, saying, "Get me this girl to be my wife."

Now Jacob heard that Shechem had defiled his daughter Dinah; but his sons were with his cattle in the field, so Jacob held his peace until they came. And Hamor the father of Shechem went out to Jacob to speak with him just as the sons of Jacob came in from the field. When they heard of it, the men were indignant and very angry, because he had committed an outrage in Israel by lying with Jacob's daughter, for such a thing ought not to be done.

But Hamor spoke with them, saying, "The heart of my son Shechem longs for your daughter; please give her to him in marriage. Make marriages with us; give your daughters to us, and take our daughters for yourselves. You shall live with us; and the land

shall be open to you; live and trade in it, and get property in it."
Shechem also said to her father and to her brothers, "Let me find
favor with you, and whatever you say to me I will give. Put the
marriage present and gift as high as you like, and I will give whatever you ask me; only give me the girl to be my wife."

The sons of Jacob answered Shechem and his father Hamor
deceitfully, because he had defiled their sister Dinah. They said to
them, "We cannot do this thing, to give our sister to one who is
uncircumcised, for that would be a disgrace to us. Only on this
condition will we consent to you: that you will become as we are
and every male among you be circumcised. Then we will give our
daughters to you, and we will take your daughters to ourselves,
and we will live among you and become one people. But if you
will not listen to us and be circumcised, then we will take our
daughter and be gone."

Their words pleased Hamor and Hamor's son Shechem. And
the young man did not delay to do the thing, because he was de-
lighted with Jacob's daughter. Now he was the most honored of all
his family. So Hamor and his son Shechem came to the gate of
their city and spoke to the men of their city, saying, "These people
are friendly with us; let them live in the land and trade in it, for
the land is large enough for them; let us take their daughters in
marriage, and let us give them our daughters. Only on this condition will the they agree to live among us, to become one people:
that every male among us be circumcised as they are circumcised.
Will not their livestock, their property, and all their animals be
ours? Only let us agree with them, and they will live among us."
And all who went out of the city gate heeded Hamor and his son
Shechem; and every male was circumcised, all who went out of
the gate of his city.

On the third day, when they were still in pain, two of the sons
of Jacob, Simeon and Levi, Dinah's brothers, took their swords
and came against the city unawares, and killed all the males. They
killed Hamor and his son Shechem with the sword, and took
Dinah out of Shechem's house, and went away. And the other
sons of Jacob came upon the slain, and plundered the city, because their sister had been defiled. They took their flocks and their
herds, their donkeys, and whatever was in the city and in the field.
All their wealth, all their little ones and their wives, all that was in

the houses, they captured and made their prey. Then Jacob said to Simeon and Levi, "You have brought trouble on me by making me odious to the inhabitants of the land, the Canaanites and the Perizzites; my numbers are few, and if they gather themselves against me and attack me, I shall be destroyed, both I and my household." But they said, "Should our sister be treated like a whore?"

— *Genesis 34 (NRSV)*

DINAH

I feel guilty because I never noticed Dinah. Years of Sunday school, a couple reads through the Bible, a year in divinity school and, still, I never noticed Dinah. I had heard of Jacob and Esau. I knew something about Leah and Rebekah. I knew that Jacob wrestled at Penuel and became "Israel." I knew that the twelve tribes of Israel were named after Jacob's sons. But I completely missed Dinah. Dinah. Dee-nah. "Dee-nah," say my friends who know Hebrew. In Hebrew, there is no long "i" sound in "Dinah," like we want to say. Her friends and her siblings would have called her "Dee-nah."

Dinah is Jacob's baby girl. She's Leah's only daughter. She is almost an afterthought when mentioned in the thirty-first chapter of Genesis. But Genesis 34 tells part of her story. She was raped by Shechem and negotiated for a bride price. She was avenged by her brothers and later blamed for poor international relations. Her story is part and parcel of the family tales and soap-opera–like dramas that make up the life of the patriarchs and matriarchs we read about and embrace as part of our Jewish and Christian heritage. But I missed her.

I missed her because I had never heard a sermon about Dinah. I missed her because there were no church school lessons about Dinah. I missed her because she never speaks for herself. And yet, here she is. In our tradition. In our holy book. In our spiritual heritage. She is one of many women who make up the recorded incidences of rape in the Bible. Dinah.

When we read Genesis 34, we hear about all the incidents that followed the rape of Dinah. We read about the response of her rapist, Shechem. We find out about the response of her father, Jacob. We learn about the reactions of her brothers, Simeon and Levi.

But we never hear Dinah's voice.

We never find out about what really happens with Dinah. She disappears from our scriptural heritage just as silently as she entered it. I missed it completely, and it troubles me.

So it seems appropriate to name a church response after Dinah because she is so silent and so overlooked, and yet she is one of us. We are silent about the crisis of sexual violence. We overlook the pain of the victims and victimizers in our midst. We respond with silence, anger, violence, and bargaining, but we don't stop and notice our own Dinahs.

How might our spiritualities be different if we had noticed Dinah the way we notice Abraham and Isaac, Jacob and Moses? What kind of questions might we ask? What did Dinah feel? What would Dinah have said? What would Dinah have liked for her community to do? Where was Dinah's God in her pain? What might Dinah have asked for? What does the ancestral voice of Dinah say to me now? How, I ask myself in both shame and compassion, did I miss Dinah?

A church response to sexual violence owns the fact that sometimes we miss our Dinahs, but we don't want to. It strives to give voice and response to the stories we don't always hear about. A church response acknowledges the ugliness in our tradition, and looks within that same tradition for hope and healing.

A church response to sexual violence must also be careful not to do to our own Dinahs what was done to the biblical Dinah. It's easy to be angry and want to seek revenge. It's easy to get caught up in learning about and negotiating the legalities and technicalities that result from the experiences of sexual violence. When we learn more about sexual violence, it is easy for us to assume that we know what needs to be done and to make sure it happens. When we do these things, we are no better than Dinah's brothers, her father, and Shechem's family. A church response is attentive to our Dinahs. We must see Dinah as the real live people in our midst. We have to talk with our Dinahs. We need to sit with our Dinahs through their pain. We need to ask our Dinahs what it is they have experienced, and with what they still struggle. We need to be for our Dinahs what the biblical Dinah did not have. We need to ask our Dinahs what they want and what they need.

4

some basic information

knew what most people know about rape: it's bad. I watched too many movies where women were walking alone at night in dark parking structures. From the shadows appears a man in a ski mask with a knife. The eerie music comes on and we all know what is about to happen. This was my picture of rape. I now know how inadequate and simple my understanding was.

We have to know more than we know now. One of the greatest problems surrounding a popular response to sexual violence is the misinformation that many of us possess about rape, incest, child molestation, and sexual assault. This lack of popular information is even more challenging for faith communities. For churches to respond to sexual violence, we must have some basic knowledge of the effects of sexual violence and, specifically, of the spiritual and religious effects of sexual violence. Learning basic information about sexual violence is the way that we begin to listen to our Dinahs.

Sexual violence, in its broadest sense, includes nonconsensual and some seemingly consensual relations. *Sexual assault* is nonconsensual, sexual violation, including rape and nonpenetrating acts such as touching, groping, undressing, sucking, kissing, and the coercion to look at sexually.

Rape is nonconsensual vaginal, anal, or oral penetration with a penis, finger, or other foreign object. *Acquaintance rape* is rape by someone known; *stranger rape* is rape by someone who is unknown. *Date rape* is rape by someone with whom there is an ongoing relationship. *Gang rape* is rape by two or more persons; *marital rape* is rape by a spouse. *Incest* is sexual assault or rape by a family member. *Child sexual abuse* is sexual assault or rape of anyone under eighteen.

Seemingly consensual sexual relations of unequal power dimensions are also sexually violent. Examples of this type of violation are military rank, teacher-student, employer-employee, counselor-client, attorney-client, clergy-parishioner, and the like. All of these definitions fall under the rubric of sexual violence. This book will focus almost exclusively on nonconsensual sexual violence, giving special attention to the fact that 85 to 90 percent of the incidents of sexual violence are committed by persons who were known, loved, or trusted prior to the assault.

Sexual violence is a *crime of violence*. This seemingly simple statement can be credited to the work of feminists who have worked to show that sexual violence is not just a sexual act. Sexual violence is a violent crime that uses and abuses sexuality to assert power and control. It is always important to remember that sexual violence occurs to girls, boys, and men, as well as women.

There are many people who are involved in the experience of sexual violence, so that terminology has become an important issue. Many people feel that the term "victim" cripples the person who has been violated. It refers to someone's entire personhood as if s/he is and always will be powerless and hurt—a "victim." Others prefer the term "survivor" as an indication that the "victim" has survived the attack and is now living in the world trying to put life back together. Some will combine both terms saying "victim-survivor." Still others use the term "thriver" to indicate that there is a full life after assault. The people who have been hurt are not victims, and have done more than survived with the bare bones of existence around them. Indeed, it is possible to enjoy life, to thrive, after assault. Similarly, the people who have committed sexual violence are variously referred to as "perpetrators," "offenders," "rapists," and "violators." No one term sums up the experience of the persons who have been hurt or the people who are violating. I tend to use all of these terms interchangeably. I also use the long phrase: "those who have experienced sexual violence." By this, I intend to focus on the victim while also remembering that sexual violence causes pain for many other people as

well—family, friends, social communities—anyone who loves and cares
for the victim or perpetrator.

In order to understand the spiritual and religious dimensions of sexual
violence, it is important to understand the emotional and psychological
effects of sexual violence. Oftentimes, the emotional trauma contributes
to the spiritual trauma that is also experienced by victims of sexual violence. Scholars have identified a series of aftereffects of the experiences of
sexual violence that is specifically traumatic. This trauma has been called
"rape trauma syndrome" and "post-traumatic stress disorder."

In the mid 1970s, Ann Burgess and Lynda Holstrom identified "rape
trauma syndrome." In their landmark work, *Rape: Victims of Crisis*,
Burgess and Holstrom considered rape trauma in two phases: acute and
long-term. The immediate response within days or weeks of the event elic-
its the following responses: expressed (angry, fearful, anxious, tearful) or
controlled (masked, hidden, calm, composed) emotions, physical symptoms of pain, sleep disturbances, eating disturbances, emotions of fear, humiliation, degradation, guilt, shame, embarrassment, self-blame, anger or
revenge, or irritability. A victim-survivor may try to block the remembrance of the incident from the memory, or the victim may continually rethink how the situation might have been avoided.

The long-term process may take from months to years. Victims may
change lifestyles by interrupting their routines, turning to family or friends,
getting away, moving, changing locks or phone numbers. Dreams and
nightmares may persist. The victim may have sudden pronounced fear of
crowds, or of being alone, or of odors of things associated with the rape.
The individual may be paranoid or suspicious of close friends or forces in
the world. Relationships will be disturbed by fear of sex, decreased sexual
desire, feelings of loneliness, and uncertainty about future relationships.

In the early 1990s, Judith Lewis Herman pushed the envelope one step
further. She asserted that sexual violence not only produces its own unique
sets of traumatic responses, as earlier indicated, but it actually begins the
onset of post-traumatic stress disorder (PTSD). In *Trauma and Recovery:
The Aftermath of Violence*, Herman compares the experiences of political
terror to that of domestic abuse. The same disorder that plagues veterans
of war and political prisoners is the same experience of those who have
survived sexual violence. Herman describes PTSD in this manner:

For many victims, the first response to sexual violence is to remain
silent about the experience. Shortly after the incident, the victim experiences a fear as great as a terror. Victims will be on permanent alert as if

danger might return at any moment. They will startle easily, overreact to small stimuli, or experience anxiety attacks around men, adults, or anything else that reminds them of the attack. The experience will constantly intrude into the victim's life in the form of flashbacks and nightmares. These intrusions have the same emotional intensity of the original event. On an emotional level, there is virtually no distinction between those who have experienced attempted rape or actual rape. The physical and ontological assault has been made in the attempt alone. It is also not unusual for the victim to demonstrate dissociative behavior. In such instances, the victim will appear indifferent, emotionally detached, or passive. This dissociative behavior is an inward attempt to protect oneself from unbearable pain. The terror is characterized by behavior wherein the victim expresses extreme emotions at one moment and detachment and withdrawal the next. Chronic trauma resulting from the incident includes psychosomatic reactions, intense fear of repeated abuse, a solitary inner life, and extremely limited goals and views of the future. Basic trust is problematic, and the victim seems to be clingy or withdrawn in interpersonal relationships. The image of the body is irrevocably altered.

The recovery process falls within three stages: safety, remembrance and mourning, and reconnection. It is important for the victim to name the problem. This gives the victim a language for the experience. If victims are informed about the traumatic symptoms, they will be less frightened when they occur. This way, the victim will understand the behavior as normal rather than "crazy." Victims will need to reestablish control over their bodies through proper medical care, the restoration of biological rhythms of eating and sleep, and the reduction of hyperarousal and intrusive symptoms. The victim will also need to establish a safe environment for residence and existence.

The same pain and trauma that has commonly been associated with veterans of the Vietnam War is the same pain and trauma that many individuals silently suffer in our churches every week. It is startling, scary, and yet incredibly eye-opening. The same experiences that have emotional dimensions also have corollary spiritual dimensions: to feel that one's life is threatened, to feel dirty, to feel angry, to feel guilty, to feel vengeful, to experience suffering. These feelings directly relate to our experiences with God and the Christian tradition.

For many victims, the experience of sexual violence is *life-threatening*. In fact, many of the symptoms of the emotional trauma are an acute stress reaction to the threat of being killed. It is as if there has been a close encounter with death and the survivor is just lucky to be alive. Facing death is always a spiritual issue. Churches readily acknowledge this when we speak of eternal life. We readily acknowledge this when we organize and attend funerals. The tension between fear of death and the promise of eternal life is central to much of Christian thought.

A feeling of *dirtiness* also tends to accompany the experience of sexual violence. Feelings of dirtiness are spiritual issues. The perceived needs for cleansing demonstrates the sense of dirty skin, but also a dirty soul. When one's sexuality and right to consent are taken away, that which is intended for sacrality has been made vile and disgusting. There may remain a disdain for the body that is connected to the religious tradition of punishing or submitting the body in order to elevate the soul. This feeling of an "unclean soul" demonstrates the way in which the body and the soul are connected. Sexual violence violates both the body and the spirit.

The intense *anger* that often accompanies experiences of sexual violence is also a religious issue. The biblical tradition often teaches us to "be angry but do not sin" (Eph. 4:26). This passage is often interpreted as an admonition against anger by equating anger with sin. In reality, anger is a natural and healthy response to violence. There is a distinct difference between vengeance and righteous indignation. Revenge easily becomes self-destructive. If vengeance is harbored inside, it will eat away at the soul in similar ways as does sin. If vengeance is enacted in vigilante or legal arenas, individuals may end up imprisoned themselves or frustrated if legal findings do not instantly produce peace and healing. Righteous indignation, on the other hand, is healthy and seeks justice. The example of Jesus' anger at the moneychangers in the temple (John 2:14–17) is a phenomenal example of righteous indignation in the Christian tradition.

Many victims feel as though they are the ones who have *sinned*. When they feel guilt, self-blame, anger, or any of the other effects of the trauma, they may perceive that they have sinned against themselves, God, or others. The issue of sin has always been one with which religious communities have wrestled and which they have addressed.

The Christian edict of *forgiveness* is always difficult for the victim of abuse. Oftentimes forgiveness is defined as "forgive and forget" or "pretend the abuse never happened." Neither option is really possible for the victim. The abuse will never be forgotten. It is a part of the person's history. On the other hand, many psychological professionals will assert that a victim does not need to forgive. For the Christian victim of sexual violence raised to believe that forgiveness is a necessary component in relating to God and others, this is not an option either. This tension surrounding forgiveness is a key spiritual struggle in the experience of sexual violence.

The most salient spiritual, religious, and philosophical dilemma concerns *suffering*. Individuals often feel as if God has abandoned them in the event of suffering. Many people express difficulty with prayer or attending church after experiencing a great suffering from which God did not deliver them. Some people feel as though their suffering is God's punishment for prior sin or a lack of faith. Some people feel as though God did not protect them from suffering. Some people feel that God brought the attack on as a test of faith or a lesson to teach them something. There are no perfect or adequate answers to the question that always arises for those in the crisis of sexual violence: "God, why did this happen to me?"

The anger, the fear, the guilt, and the suffering belong to the entire community. When sexual violence comes to the forefront of our minds, everyone feels a little less safe. Everyone becomes a little less trustworthy. Everyone has the right to a little more anger. Everyone feels the vulnerability to the intensity of suffering. For this reason, it is important to highlight the fact that sexual violence affects more than those whom we traditionally think of as the obvious victims. Sexual violence affects the entire community. Sexual violence affects the individual who is violated, the individual who perpetrated the violence, and anyone who loves either one of them. The pain, the shame, the confusion, and the anger evoked by this type of violence affect everyone in a community. While the trauma is unique for the person who has been violated, we must remember that many perpetrators were once violated themselves. We must remember that the community's silence has left all of us ill equipped to respond to, love, care for, and restore the brokenness that the experience of sexual violence can leave in its path. We must remember that all of us need community, compassion, and support to deal with the most difficult moments in our lives. The crisis of sexual violence is no different. When we think of sexual violence as a community issue, we are forced to understand that the face of sexual violence is everyone's face.

When we understand the specifically religious and spiritual dimensions to the experience of sexual violence, we understand that the call to address sexual violence is a call to churches. The crisis of sexual violence calls all churches to do something. It calls all churches to say something. It calls all churches to offer something that only they can offer: a voice for the presence of God in the midst of this crisis.

The Dinah Project is an organized church response to the crisis of sexual violence in our communities. It is an attempt to say and do something. It is not a ministry with the answers, but a ministry that is willing to wrestle with the questions. In this book, I share how one church began to give Dinah a face, a name, a community, a worship service, and even a sermon.

5

doing your homework

I admit it. I'm a natural student. Research is what I do. I enjoy wandering around in libraries. I like the smell of old books. I am used to looking for information. But I do get tired of it sometimes. I know I need more information, but I don't know where and how to get it. And when I do, finding out what I need requires reading and learning a lot of useless information before I get to the part that I want to know. Sometimes I just want the Cliffs Notes version on critical issues. I want someone else to tell me the important things and leave out the stuff I don't need to know.

With sexual violence, doing homework on the front end saves from having test anxiety on the back end. For many of the questions I had, experienced social workers already had the answers. For all the issues I was about to encounter in my desire to "start a new ministry," many existing agencies were confronting them every day. I had already found the local rape and sexual abuse center when I started the ministry. It was there that I received my own counseling. So I naturally began with them when I needed information. My former therapist became my primary informant. Using that technique over and over, I acquired the ability to provide information to other people almost immediately after they asked me for it.

The first step is getting to know your community. The first step in addressing the crisis of sexual violence is finding out who else in your community is already working on these issues. You will probably be unwilling and/or unable to provide comprehensive legal, psychological, and medical care from your church's ministry. And there is no need to reinvent the wheel if these services are already being provided in your community. If this is the only step you take in addressing sexual violence through your church, this is the most important one. Learning your community will allow you to develop three key aspects of your ministry:

- A referral list
- Personal relationships with service providers
- Knowledge of the impact of sexual violence in your local community

If someone comes to you with an issue of sexual violence, you don't have to be an expert, but it will be helpful to have resources for that person to access. If you have met with individuals in these agencies, you can always use your name as a contact and follow-up to make sure people have their needs met. An individual will often feel much better about calling an unknown person with the delicate issues that they are dealing with, if they feel that you already know and trust the person or agency. If you refer people, it's also nice to offer to accompany individuals on their first trip to the agency.

FIND OUT ABOUT EXISTING SERVICES

If you are interested in developing a larger ministry within your church, you will want to know where the gap in services exists and try to see how you can fill that gap. Perhaps there are few services that are free of charge. Or perhaps there are few services that are culturally sensitive. Perhaps there are no services that currently address sexual violence from a faith perspective. The only way to know if there is even a need for different types of services is to know what your community is currently offering.

Find out if your community has any type of *rape crisis center*. Start with "R" in the phone book. Look for "rape." Also try calling the Rape, Abuse & Incest National Network (RAINN) hotline number 800-656-HOPE. This national hotline connects callers with the closest rape crisis center based on the area code from which they are calling. Although you may not want to tie up a crisis line with administrative questions, learn the appropriate number to call, the best time to call, and the person to whom you should speak to find out about the services that are provided in your area. Ask about the demographics of the population that is being served. Many rape crisis centers also have a speakers' bureau that lists people who are willing to give lectures on sexual violence or share from their own experiences as survivors. When I served on the speakers' bureau of my local crisis center, I was willing to talk to just about anybody and answer any questions. Be sure to ask if there might be a therapist or survivor willing to meet with you and answer any questions you might have.

Call the *police department* and ask about the procedures that they use with victims and perpetrators of sexual assault. Try to make an appointment with an officer to get information and referrals to any special departments that may exist within your local police force. Many police departments have specialized assistance for victims of crime, free counseling, advocacy, and similar services. How are minor victims and assailants of the crime treated? Is there a special juvenile court and system? This is also a good time to ask about medical services for victims of sexual assault.

Procedures for immediate *medical services* for victims of sexual assault are not as straightforward as it might appear. There is a certain type of training needed to administer a rape kit. Rape kits gather the particular information used in legal cases. Sometimes there are only a couple individuals that service a community or only one or two particular hospitals that are equipped to collect this particular kind of data. Some hospital personnel are not trained to do rape kits but will see patients after assaults to monitor their health and safety. Learn the procedure in your community.

Look in some of the *less-obvious places.* Look for organizations and individuals who work with populations that may also have a high incidence of the experience of sexual violence. Look at programs that work with recovering addicts from drugs and alcohol, prostitution, incarcerated populations or those recently released from incarceration, persons living with HIV/ AIDS, homeless populations, domestic violence programs, the security department of local college campuses. Clients of these programs may not seek assistance related to the experience of sexual violence, but those who work in these programs often testify that sexual assault, rape and incest are often part of the history of many clients. Some programs may already offer services to address these needs of their clients; they may partner with other local agencies; or they may be looking for assistance in meeting these needs of their clients.

DEVELOP RELATIONSHIPS WITH PROVIDERS

After the initial call, try to meet with someone in person. This will give you an opportunity to visit the center, see the facilities, and indicate your commitment to learning about the agency. Even if a face-to-face appointment is unavailable, try to get answers to these questions over the phone:

- Do you have literature I can take with me?
- What books or articles would you recommend that I read?
- Are your services free and open to the public?
- Are there other agencies or individuals in the community that also address this need?
- Are juvenile victims and violators treated any differently?
- What is your policy on confidentiality?
- What percentage of the population you serve indicates experience as a victim or violator of sexual violence? (if this agency does not deal explicitly with sexual violence)
- Are there any recurring spiritual issues that you hear in your work? How do you address those?
- Do you have special professional or volunteer training that I can attend?
- Is there anyone in a speakers' bureau who might be willing to talk with me and answer questions?

UNDERSTAND THE IMPACT OF SEXUAL VIOLENCE

The next part of research is learning more about sexual violence in general, and the theological and spiritual impact of sexual violence in particular. There are several ways to gather this information:

- Training with community organizations
- Reading print and Internet resources
- Attending conferences

Rape crisis centers and other *community organizations* often offer very thorough training for volunteers that can give you a good understanding of the effects of sexual violence, ways to respond to victims and violators, and the procedures that are used in your particular community. Try working a crisis hotline or volunteering to accompany victims to the hospital. This will allow you to see and hear up close and personal the crises and trauma associated with the experience of sexual violence. All the literature will have a voice, a face, and a story. Volunteering or participating in the training will also help you to develop relationships with your local service agencies. The community will know that you are serious in your commitment to responding to sexual violence. Most importantly, training with local organizations may be the fastest and most intensive way to gather the information you desire.

It is also important to know the *literature in the field.* You may want to consider keeping a video, audio, and print library for the church and other persons involved in your ministry. There will be a more thorough listing of resources at the end of the book. The first of two books I recommend is *Trauma and Recovery* by Judith Lewis Herman. This is a thorough and accessible description of post-traumatic stress disorder and the steps in the healing process. You don't have to be a psychology major to understand Herman's text, but it will give you an entrée into the language and processes of the discussions on sexual violence. Understanding the response and healing process for victims of sexual violence gives greater understanding and compassion as you interact with people who are in the various stages of their healing. You can assure others that they are not insane or alone. We are all in the process of healing.

I also recommend *Sexual Violence* by Marie Fortune. In this book, Marie Fortune, a leading author on the religious impact of sexual violence, lays out many of the most critical spiritual issues that emanate from the experience of sexual violence. She speaks of church responses to victims, violators, and the entire congregation. Although she and other writers elaborate on different theological and ethical issues surrounding sexual violence in other works, this one book is my favorite introduction.

Do not neglect the *Internet* as a resource. Connect to national agencies that are working to respond to sexual violence. Read about the organizations that are responding to sexual violence from a spiritual perspective. Most importantly, the Internet can provide the most up-to-date statistics on sexual violence in your nation and in your local community. While statistics only have a certain level of accuracy, it is an important starting place for realizing the breadth and depth of this crisis in our communities.

If you are able, attend some of the *conferences* that deal explicitly with faith and sexuality. Connect with the Faith/Trust Institute (formerly the Center for the Prevention of Sexual and Domestic Violence) in Seattle, Washington; the Interfaith Sexual Trauma Institute (ISTI) in Collegeville, Minnesota; Tamar's Voice in Irvine, California; or the Religious Coalition for Reproductive Choice (RCRC) in Washington, D.C. These four organizations hold regular conferences that include faith responses to clergy sexual misconduct, sexual violence, and domestic violence. They draw speakers from across the country and across faith and denominational lines to speak on different approaches in addressing sexual violence. Some conferences include certified training and continuing education units (CEUs) as well as a plethora of information and networking opportunities with others who are at work in the field across the country.

If you begin and end your response to sexual violence with research, you have done a tremendous service to your church and your community. Education and commitment to the issue are more than half the battle. Place literature you gather around your church. Place it in the library, the newsletter, the bulletin boards, or the restrooms. It is critical to place information in locations that visibly indicate your commitment to addressing sexual violence, while also giving individuals access to that information with a modicum of privacy. Because there is still so much silence and shame associated with sexual violence, some people may feel embarrassed writing down a number or address from a bulletin board. Perhaps they are willing to write the number down in a restroom, or from a church newsletter.

Some short-term ways to address sexual violence in your congregation are:

- Educate yourself about sexual violence and the spiritual effects it has upon a community.
- Write an article in your church newsletter. Include phone numbers to call.
- Make additions to the church library with pamphlets and books.
- Attach pamphlets and flyers to the bulletin board.
- Put information about counseling services and crisis hotlines in discrete locations such as restrooms.
- Invite workers from local agencies to conduct brief workshops at your church.
- Invite members of the church to volunteer with local agencies.
- Donate money to nonprofit agencies working to respond to sexual violence in your community.
- Encourage a group of church members or a particular church organization to attend a rally or event that addresses sexual violence in your community, such as Take Back the Night rallies.

Let it be known within your church and community that you care about the souls and spirits of those affected by rape, sexual assault, and incest. Taking any of these steps will help your church become a safe place for those who are wrapped up in the experience of sexual violence.

6

getting organized

I was not very organized when I began The Dinah Project. I had no idea what I was doing. I had never seen it done before and I didn't know whom to ask for help and what to ask people to do if they wanted to help. I ended up being a one-woman show much more than I should have. I was tired, scattered, and frustrated.

The good news is that I eventually figured out what to do. I made a list of what I was doing and realized that most of those things did not require my particular personality to get done. I welcomed the generosity of others and realized that a program that could easily operate on two hundred thousand dollars per year could also be done with a thousand dollars per year. Teamwork and concern for the issue are enough to begin putting a solid organizational structure in place.

Learn from my mistake. It is preferable to establish the organizational component of this ministry earlier rather than later. Although organizational structure may change with the success of the ministry, community requests for service, and additional funding, it is important to involve the membership of the church in this ministry from the beginning.

Whether the ministry begins and ends with researching the responses of sexual violence in the local community, or whether it offers more comprehensive care through worship, community education, group counseling, and collaborations with other community agencies, several minds at work are always better than one.

The Dinah Project uses an advisory committee of diverse individuals to bring direction and various gifts to the ministry. The advisory committee brings together church members from various fields that have an interest in the work of addressing sexual violence from a faith perspective. Having an advisory committee not only involves a broad cross-section of the church in the planning of this ministry, but it prevents one person from taking sole responsibility for all the activities of the ministry.

SELECTING COMMITTEE MEMBERS

The pastor of the church and a staff minister or church member who seems to be committed to addressing sexual violence should take time to identify persons within the church who may be uniquely skilled, gifted, and committed to working on this ministry.

There is no magical number of individuals who should comprise a committee, but The Dinah Project invites fifteen individuals to serve on the committee, knowing that some will be unwilling or unable to serve in this capacity. Seek out individuals who:

- Have interest in the topic of addressing sexual violence

- Have an area of expertise that will benefit the ministry

- Represent different experiences of life in the world and church

Some people will automatically come to mind when beginning to address the topic of sexual violence. I began by talking to an active member of the congregation who is also a psychiatrist. I asked her if she was interested and knew other people who might be. We sat down and brainstormed about other people. There may be individuals who openly discuss their experiences of sexual violence and are actively looking for ways to speak out against rape, incest, and child sexual abuse. Others may have confided interest in this issue to clergy. Some individuals responded positively to brochures and information that had been placed throughout the church. If there are no persons who have obvious commitments to addressing sexual violence, imagine what persons may be interested in learning more and being involved. Think of persons who work with children or populations with addictions, those in social work, or those involved in law enforcement and issues of violence in general. These same people may have interest in addressing sexual violence in particular.

Board members may also represent different areas of expertise that will be needed as the ministry grows. Look for individuals who:

- Enjoy research

- Have grant-writing or budgeting skills

- Have creative or dramatic skills

- Demonstrate a commitment to health issues

- Possess a background in social work or psychology

- Work with children through education or juvenile justice work

- Work with populations that may contain a high percentage of those who are victims or perpetrators of sexual violence

These persons can be instrumental in coordinating worship services, seeking funds, and bringing a specialized perspective to the church's growing knowledge about the impact of sexual violence in the local community.

The committee should be as diverse as the members of the church and community. Be sure the committee is composed of persons of varying ages, genders, races, and experiences. Be intentional about asking a young adult and teenager to serve on the board. Be sure the committee is not composed entirely of women. Some committee members' personal or professional experiences are their greatest contributions to the ministry. Choose individuals from various socioeconomic classes and educational backgrounds. Our committee ended up with a retired social worker, a woman who specializes in writing grants for nonprofit agencies, another woman who works with recovering drug addicts, a defense attorney, a teenage survivor of incest, a psychiatrist, and a graphic artist who wanted to help in any way.

Invite members to a meeting where they can meet each other and learn about the ministry's idea and goals. Ask potential members to think about their own ideas for the ministry and the ways in which they can contribute. Send out a written letter of invitation, but also call persons individually to talk with them about their interest in serving on the committee. Tell them why they were selected and how important their presence would be to the ministry.

While talking with potential members, listen to see what persons seem particularly excited about and committed to this ministry. One of these people may be willing to serve as the chairperson for the committee. The chairperson will help to organize meetings and maintain the passion for the work on the advisory committee.

THE COMMITTEE'S TASKS

The advisory committee has the potential to be intimately involved in the regular activities of the ministry, or it can contribute as needs arise. Oftentimes, the different tasks that are needed can be done by one or two individuals working on a particular assignment for a limited period of time. Again, this prevents any one person from feeling overburdened and overwhelmed.

The advisory committee can be responsible for the following activities:

- Developing vision and mission statements
- Designing a logo or promotional materials
- Conducting a needs assessment
- Providing artistic or clinical support
- Helping to coordinate volunteers
- Keeping archives of the ministry
- Seeking funding for the ministry

DEVELOPING VISION AND MISSION STATEMENTS

One of the first projects for the advisory committee can be the development of a name, and vision and mission statements. You may want to use the name "The Dinah Project," or there may be another name that seems to embody the spirit of tradition, the ministry, and the local church. Draw upon those creative persons for ideas and form.

The vision statement talks about the ideal environment. The mission statement discusses the way in which this particular ministry will work towards that vision. Consider using an outside consultant who specializes in organizational management. Perhaps a member of the church or community can volunteer a couple hours of guidance in developing vision and mission statements. Check with local career agencies for these individuals. If that person is not available, check the library and Internet. There are several resources that assist people in developing personal and organizational mission statements.

DESIGNING A LOGO OR PROMOTIONAL MATERIALS

Again, you may want to work with the creative members of the committee to develop a logo and promotional materials for the ministry. Perhaps there is a graphic artist on the committee or in the church or community who may be willing to give some time and energy to the design of these items. Once they are done, they can be used over and over again during worship events and community education sessions.

CONDUCTING A NEEDS ASSESSMENT

An important part of starting a ministry that addresses sexual violence is researching the community. This need not be the task of one individual. A team of persons can divide the research and report back to each other and the committee about the lessons they have learned. While doing this research, they will be doing an informal needs assessment.

- Where are the gaps in services?
- What are the expressed needs that are not being met?
- Which of these needs do we have the capacity to address and how can we do that?

This last question will be the critical question for the committee. It will quickly become clear that all of the committee's ideas cannot be implemented and all of the community's needs cannot be met. It is the role of the committee to determine what the local church can do with the resources it possesses or can obtain.

PROVIDING ARTISTIC OR CLINICAL SUPPORT

The committee's members with specialized gifts and skills in the arts and social work or psychotherapy will prove invaluable to the ministry. Creative individuals may take responsibility for the litanies, poems, or dramas that compose aspects of the worship events. The Dinah Project held one service entitled "Ministry Through the Arts" that drew upon various members of the local artistic community to offer presentations through the written word, dramatics, storytelling, spoken word, dance, song, and other creative expression. This event drew both the church crowd and aficionados of the arts who do not usually attend church events. It was also exciting to address sexual violence in a church in a nontraditional manner—there was never an actual sermon or homily. The personal contacts of creative members of the advisory committee were instrumental in locating different artist participants.

Any members of the committee with professional experiences as clinicians can provide guidance on the sensitive and technical issues of addressing sexual violence. This knowledge can be helpful on a case-by-case basis if leaders of the ministry need assistance helping individuals to get their needs met. The knowledge of these members is also instrumental in developing group counseling and community education.

HELPING TO COORDINATE VOLUNTEERS

As the ministry grows, many individuals may desire to participate in the program in one way or another. One committee member may be willing to serve as a volunteer coordinator by helping to maintain contact with volunteers, compiling volunteer logs, and suggesting different ways in which persons can volunteer. Whatever the budget of the ministry, communal support and participation are instrumental to the success of the project. But volunteer coordination can quickly become overwhelming if there is not an individual in place to work with volunteers as they contribute.

KEEPING THE ARCHIVES OF THE MINISTRY

There should be at least one person who maintains updated paperwork and documentation for the activities of the ministry. Everything from newspaper clippings to press releases to worship guides/printed bulletins from worship services to announcements in the church newsletter can be included in the archives. Anything that is printed or recorded under the auspices of the ministry should be compiled in triplicate. One copy should stay at the church at all times. Another copy may be circulated, and the last and most updated copy will be in the hands of the archivist.

Documenting the ministry is important for the church's own archives, but it also allows the ministry to see how far it has come and what has been accomplished. The committee may wish to set different goals for each year of the ministry. The documenting of the ministry helps to remind committee members of what has been accomplished in a year's time.

SEEKING FUNDING FOR THE MINISTRY

Anyone who works in development or grant writing can tell you that fund-raising is a full-time job. The ministry can depend heavily on volunteers and support from the church. As the ministry grows, it will require additional funds to implement its programs. What seems like excessive documentation will come in handy when the ministry decides to seek external funding.

Committee members with experience in fund-raising can be incredibly helpful at this time. There are federal funds that are set aside for agencies that respond to sexual violence. There are also private corporations who seek to underwrite cultural or educational events in local communities. Persons from the committee can learn what is needed to be eligible for federal funds—for example, nonprofit status or internal audits. They can also make contacts with federal or state agencies that distribute these funds and search the Internet for foundations with sensitivities to efforts that respond to sexual violence. Remember that sexual violence may fall under the category of "women's issues," "health," and "violence."

After the committee has met, and individuals have made a commitment to serving in this capacity, be certain to gather resumes of all committee members. This documenting effort will be useful when applying for grants and evaluating the skills and gifts of persons involved in the ministry.

ADDITIONAL STAFF PERSONS

The committee may find it necessary to hire, appoint, or select additional staff persons. Whether or not the funding exists to give these individuals a competitive salary, The Dinah Project has identified positions that help to run the ministry. Until funding exists, clergy members or volunteers from the church or community may fill the positions. (See appendix B for job descriptions.)

Do not feel overwhelmed! A church response to sexual violence can be a two hundred thousand dollar per year program with staff, facilities, advisory committees, and large granting sources. It can also be the effort of concerned individuals and volunteers to make a difference in the local community. In fact, this is the only way the ministry can begin. Good planning and collective input can help to make one worship service more effective. Realize that developing a ministry that addresses sexual violence will not happen overnight, nor will it necessarily happen in the sequence that this book suggests. Many of these activities will occur simultaneously. For example, the first worship service can be held before a mission statement is written. Group counseling can be done without full-time staff members. The most important component of the ministry is the commitment of the church and community to creating safe places for healing from the pain of sexual violence.

7

saying "rape" in the sanctuary: *worship*

I don't know if my pastor ever used the word "rape" when he preached, or made announcements about The Dinah Project. He, like so many of us, found numerous euphemisms to avoid saying "rape." He said, "the experience of intimate violence," "deep personal pain," and "despairing conditions." I understand that it is hard. Worship is supposed to feel good, and "rape" does not bring warm, fuzzy feelings. Worship is supposed to be about praising God, and "rape" does not make anyone want to celebrate. Worship is supposed to be about bringing communities together, and "rape" makes us feel alone and isolated.

Someone had to say it. Someone had to use "the r-word" in the sanctuary. Because rape is just as much a part of reality as eating, drinking, singing, dancing, kneeling, sitting and listening—all the things we are used to doing at church. Saying "rape" in the sanctuary requires boldness and creativity. It means finding a way to talk about the emotions that result from the experience of sexual violence. It is naming the sin in our midst and fighting against it.

I came to realize that my pastor didn't have to say the word "rape" for the ministry to be successful. I used the word "rape." I found outside preachers who boldly cited Scripture and reminded us that the stories were stories of rape. I found youth who were willing to recite poems and participate in dramatizations that described hopelessness and sadness. I found litanies that talked about God's presence in the midst of all pain. These are the entry points. Entering through them, I found worship to be richer and more diverse than ever.

Worship is the starting and ending point of our Christian ministries. Worship allows us to turn our faces from ourselves and towards God. In the worship moment, we highlight God's activity in the world and its saving power for our congregations and the wider community. Worship has the power to unify persons who might not otherwise come together. More than any other aspect of church life, worship focuses on God, rather than the characteristics of race, class, gender, and other issues that typically fragment and divide our communities. In liturgies, communal prayer, song, preaching, and sacrament, we ritually and regularly surrender ourselves to the glory of God in our midst.

What better arena for a church to address the crisis of sexual violence than in a worship setting? What better place to remind our communities that God is not silent and uncaring in our deepest trials? What better place to reinforce the love, presence, and healing power of God than in worship?

The *purpose* of addressing sexual violence in worship is

- To raise community awareness of sexual violence
- To be a voice for the presence of God in the midst of the crisis of sexual violence
- To wrestle with the most challenging spiritual questions that accompany the experience of sexual violence
- To open the church as a safe place for our Dinahs—those needing refuge, compassion, and healing from the experience of sexual violence

Addressing sexual violence through worship involves more planning than does the average worship service. It requires a level of intentionality and creativity that usually do not seem necessary with other worship events. To dare to combine the words "sex" and "violence" and the pulpit is no easy task. Planning, creativity, and prayer can make for several successful ways of combining worship and the crises of rape, sexual abuse, and incest.

The Dinah Project has identified ten areas of attention for coordinating worship services that address sexual violence.

1. Choose a theme for the service.

2. Identify a time and date for each service.

3. Be traditional with a lot of creativity.

4. Find a preacher.

5. Remove barriers that might prevent people from coming.

6. Provide aftercare for issues that arise.

7. Use publicity effectively

8. Video-/audiotape the service.

9. Develop a budget.

10. Utilize volunteer activity.

CHOOSE A THEME

Since sexual violence is a deep and broad subject area with several underlying issues and subtopics, the best way to frame a worship service is by picking a single theme of focus. The Dinah Project uses three themes for three worship services to occur in one single year. We revolve these themes, sticking with these three basic topics.

Theme 1: Community Recognition

By beginning with community recognition, the church is calling persons to understand sexual violence as the community's issue. The communal setting of worship reinforces this assertion. With this theme, several educational elements can be introduced to give basic information about sexual violence, definitions, statistics, the effects, and so on. This can also be a time when different facets of the community come together to speak out against sexual violence. This theme also provides the opportunity to discuss the way in which sexual violence occurs in the Bible. It was during this theme that we did the "Ministry Through the Arts" service.

Theme 2: Forgiveness

Forgiveness between human beings is a difficult task in any context. This becomes a murky issue in the context of sexual violence because some service providers insist that a victim does not have to forgive the abuser, whereas the Christian tradition has long asserted that forgiveness of neighbor is a critical part of the Christian life. These warring opinions can cause spiritual dissonance for the entire community that does not know how to respond to the abuser in its midst. Rather than simply state some version of "Forgive and forget because God won't forgive you if you don't forgive others," this is an opportunity to wrestle with the concept of forgiveness. Help define forgiveness—what it is and what it is not. Address the biblical messages about forgiveness. Address the "when" and "how" of forgiveness. Admit that forgiveness is difficult and that it is often a long and arduous spiritual process. When we gather in worship around the theme of forgiveness, we do not claim to have the perfect answer for everyone. We do, however, promise to wrestle with it and work on it in community with the love and support of those who share the same faith. We are pledging not to ignore this aspect of our spiritualities or healing processes.

Because forgiveness is such a challenging topic, a workshop always accompanies the worship experience. This gives a workshop leader the opportunity to address the different aspects of forgiveness in a setting that allows for dialogue. Readings, handouts, and question-and-answer sessions work particularly well before or after a worship service.

Theme 3: Healing

Churches have long been associated as places to be healed from our "sin-sick souls" and the trials and tribulations of life. The wounds of sexual violence demand a type of healing that cannot occur in a hospital or therapist's office alone. They need the special touch of God to renew the damaged souls and spirits of the victims, abusers and loved ones. Many churches already have rituals to facilitate healing—such as anointing, laying on of hands, and testimony. This is the time to draw on the traditions of the church to remind the entire community that "there is a balm in Gilead," and that God's healing power is still active and working in the lives of those affected by sexual violence.

These three themes alone seem boundless. With different elements of worship, the themes of community recognition, forgiveness, and healing are not easily exhausted.

IDENTIFY A TIME AND DATE FOR EACH SERVICE

You will want to have a full three months to plan for each worship service. This will give you time to invite multiple speakers or preachers (should your first choice of speakers be unavailable or unwilling), and to bring together volunteers, creative worship elements and publicity. You may even find it helpful to plan the three worship services a year at a time.

You will also want to decide the time of your service. You may decide to use a typical Sabbath morning service for this worship event. The advantage is that most of your regular congregants will be in attendance. The disadvantage to this setting is that it may prevent you from fellowshipping with members of other churches who are attending regular services at the same time. It may also make it difficult to find speakers/preachers who may have other obligations of their own at that time.

Deciding to hold a "special service" in the evening of the Sabbath or on another evening frees up many others in the faith community to attend and participate in the worship event. Of course, this may be more inconvenient in terms of opening the church facilities again, and some people from the regular service may choose not to return to the church at a later time. We have also found it difficult to schedule services between Thanksgiving and February 28 and in the middle of the summer. There tends to be an abundance of church, community, and family events in those months that will quickly fill the schedule of community activists, speakers, and worshippers alike. In short, you will get different types of audiences depending on the time and date of the services.

BE TRADITIONAL WITH A LOT OF CREATIVITY

Churches already possess a wealth of liturgical resources for addressing community recognition, forgiveness, and healing. Churches with a denominational or local history of social justice, spiritual development, and/or Pentecostal or holiness rituals may find themselves addressing these three themes on a regular basis in a variety of settings. The Christian tradition is full of songs, hymns, liturgies, and practices that readily lend themselves to worshipping around the topic of God's presence in the midst of pain and evil. With each theme, flip through a hymnal or book of worship and imagine which hymns express the sentiment associated with the theme. Remember that sacraments may well express an underlying theme. The Eucharist can be a symbol of unity for community recognition or a symbol of forgiveness. Baptism may well symbolize new life and healing as well. Remember church traditions of laying on hands or anointing.

Use Bible studies to prepare for different themes. Remember that the Psalms often express pain, anguish, and praise. It is important to ground new and different types of worship moments in traditions that are already familiar to the church. This helps congregants to feel more comfortable with the service. More importantly, it demonstrates that community involvement, forgiveness, and healing are not themes that are foreign to the faith community. It reminds us that the church may be one of the most logical places to address sexual violence because of its history as a place of expression, healing, and renewal.

It is also important to include new elements of worship in this event. Because sexual violence is not typically addressed in church settings, it requires more creativity than the average worship service. This is the time to draw on the most creative, dramatic elements of worship in order to (1) educate while worshipping, (2) hold the attention of worshippers, and (3) involve as many different aspects of the community as possible. Use contemporary Christian songs that express the feelings you want to convey. Utilize dramatic readings, art, plays or skits, new liturgies, testimonies, or dance—anything you can think of to be effective in raising consciousness about sexual violence in your congregation. Invited speakers, print and Internet resources, community contacts, the arts community, and church members can be the most helpful resources in getting together some new aspects of worship.

Don't be afraid to think outside of the box or to involve youth. Youth may want to sing a song, recite a psalm, or organize a play or skit to express their sentiments about sexual violence. Preparing youth for their part in the worship moment is an educational opportunity for them as well. On one occasion, The Dinah Project worship service included a dramatic reading of a section of Ntozake Shange's book, *for colored girls who have considered suicide/ when the rainbow is enuf.* One of the church's teenagers did the reading. Several of her friends attended to support her and they later became interested in addressing sexual violence among their peer group. Invite adolescent therapists or rape crisis workers from the community to coordinate a rap session with youth about power and control, dating, sexuality, and respect.

FIND A PREACHER

This sounds simple enough, but it can be more difficult than it appears with the topic of sexual violence. Not all preachers feel comfortable talking about, let alone preaching about, rape, incest, and child sexual abuse. Perhaps the pastor of the church is willing to begin by serving as the first preacher. However, it is often more effective when the preacher is a guest to the church's host congregation. Some preachers feel more comfortable preaching about sexual violence outside of their home congregation; some congregations are more receptive to those who are not as familiar or well known as their regular clergy.

Perhaps you already know a minister who is passionate about issues of sexual violence and will happily come to worship with you. More than likely, you will need to do some research. Begin by looking for preachers in your community or denomination who tend to be outspoken about health issues, issues of violence or sexuality, or sexual ethics. These persons may already be familiar with the crises of sexual violence, and thus feel comfortable preaching on the topic.

Also look at the authors of books and articles that address sexual violence from a theological or ethical perspective. Many of these scholars are also preachers and workshop leaders who are willing to worship with your congregation. See what Christian writers wrestle with forgiveness or healing. Look for names at your local Christian bookstore or in Christian magazines and devotionals. You may need to contact the publisher or denominational headquarters to actually contact the individual. But start with the Internet first!

A shorter path to some of the same information can be found in some of the relationships you develop in the process of research. Ask local agencies if they know of any ministers who bring a particular sensitivity to the area. Ask agency workers if they have read anything about spiritual effects of sexual violence or about forgiveness. Who is the author? How might I contact that person? Also check with the national organizations that hold conferences. Many of the keynote speakers, workshop leaders, and attendees of these conferences are ready and willing to talk about sexual violence from the pulpit. Call the program coordinators of Faith/Trust, the Interfaith Sexual Trauma Institute (ISTI), Tamar's Voice, and the Religious Coalition for Reproductive Choice (RCRC). Check the speaker lists on their websites. (See appendix A.)

Most importantly, try to invite male and female preachers to speak about sexual violence. It is far too easy to give in to the stereotype that sexual violence is a women's issue. The Dinah Project is committed to having at least one male preacher for every cycle of the three themes. This reminds everyone in the community that sexual violence affects men and women, girls and boys. So pervasive is the idea that rape is a women's issue, that we cannot overstate the contrary. A male presence speaking about sexual violence is a good tangible reminder that sexual violence affects both genders.

REMOVE BARRIERS THAT MIGHT PREVENT PEOPLE FROM COMING

Sexual violence is a difficult topic for many people to begin to face, and this worship service may give the community the first opportunity to do so. For others, addressing the topic of sexual violence has been an ongoing issue with which they have wrestled, but there have been barriers preventing them from accessing services.

Four primary barriers are

- Negative perceptions and cost of psychological counseling
- A need for child care while accessing services
- Transportation
- Services addressing sexual violence cut into major meal times

By addressing sexual violence in the church, persons who might otherwise refuse to access traditional psychological services may now feel comfortable in a faith community. For those who believe that all healing is the byproduct of the movement of God in individual lives, psychological counseling may appear to be secular and remote. For others, there is no resistance to counseling, but the high hourly cost associated with counseling services discourages individuals from investigating free services that may be available in the community. Just by hosting the worship service, churches break down an initial barrier.

Provide childcare or activities for children. You may be able to utilize one section of the church for childcare during the service. You may want to engage youth about sexual violence while the adults are participating in the regular service. Contact service agencies to see if any therapists who usually work with children or adolescents are available to donate their time. In two hours, a trained individual can talk with children about good and bad touches and ways to respond and report. They may also know of different artistic ways the children can express what they have learned. During our "Ministry Through the Arts" service, we found a child therapist to work with our young people. She had the youth produce a tangible form of artwork called "body drawings" that they were able to present to the larger congregation at the end of the service. During their artistic time, she also taught the young people how to say "no" and how to tell an adult about things that may happen to them.

Be sure to host the service during a time when transportation is available. Host the service while bus or subway lines are still running to your building. When announcing the service, provide a contact person that people can call if they need transportation. Perhaps you can make the church van available to pick up persons who want to attend but cannot provide their own transportation. Perhaps volunteers can rally together to pick up those who are coming from around the area.

If your service cuts into any meal times, be sure to provide some type of repast for service attendees. From full catering to cookies and punch, a repast can cut the edge off of the hunger cravings service attendees may feel near the end of the service. More importantly, it gives people an opportunity to mull around after the service has ended. It can be a safe and comfortable time for persons to speak to the ministers, the invited preacher, and each other or simply to remain in the church building without feeling clearly identified as "someone who needs help." No matter how much we talk about sexual violence, there is still a large stigma associated with the experience.

PROVIDE AFTERCARE FOR ISSUES THAT ARISE

A worship service addressing sexual violence will unearth issues within individuals who should not be sent back into the world without assistance for their newly raised questions and needs. To host the worship service without preparing for the emotional needs of some attendees is spiritually irresponsible. You may find that the emotional needs of the attendees exceed the church's capacity to minister to them, but we still must prepare.

Invite therapists and agency workers with whom you are in contact. Ask if they are willing to stay after the service and answer questions that people may have. Perhaps staff ministers or prayer warriors can be available to sit and talk with people after the service. Whoever is designated as someone who is capable of handling aftercare should be clearly identified, knowledgeable of aftercare services in the community, and able to follow up with the individual later that week. The Dinah Project used white ribbons to identify those persons who made themselves available for aftercare. Purple or blue ribbons are also appropriate as purple designates those standing against domestic and sexual violence, and blue ribbons designate those standing against child abuse. These resource people may have a business card with the phone numbers of Christian counselors or rape crisis centers printed on it.

The identification of these individuals also gives volunteers and other church members an opportunity to learn about representatives from various services available in the community. The reception with identified resource persons can almost double as an information fair for the church community to learn more about the ways in which the community is already responding to sexual violence.

USE PUBLICITY EFFECTIVELY

Begin working on publicity four weeks before the worship service is scheduled to take place. Begin by collecting a black-and-white glossy picture and biographical sketch of the invited preacher. This will be important for the press release, design of the worship guide/bulletin, and the introduction of the speaker.

Gather a list of contacts for publicity efforts—all the agencies that have been contacted, other churches, local newspapers, radio stations, and so on. Take time to make a permanent list of agencies, contact persons, phone numbers, fax numbers, and e-mail addresses. When the press release is written, a volunteer can fax, mail, or hand deliver the information. Call radio stations and ask for the fax number and contact person for community service announcements. Check with the local paper and establish a relationship with the religion editor or community events editor. Always provide a black-and-white picture with the press release for newspapers. Press releases need to go out a minimum of two weeks before the worship event.

Flyer design can occur hand in hand with the press release. The flyers can be distributed and posted at local churches, community centers, and agencies. Although flyers and press releases are important means of publicity, the best means is word of mouth. Be sure to follow up on the phone or in person with agency representatives and other churches. With a topic as challenging as sexual violence, the best publicity efforts can generate a relatively small crowd. Don't be discouraged. Keep in mind that addressing rape, incest, and child abuse in the church may still be revolutionary for your community. Remember how difficult it is for our loved ones, our neighbors, and ourselves to face these issues. Consistency in holding services and generating publicity will prove your dedication to the community at large regardless of the number of people who attend the event.

VIDEO-/AUDIOTAPE THE SERVICE

Recording the service is important for the archives of the church, but also for continued ministry of this effort. Audio- and videotapes can reach persons who were unable to attend the service, those outside of your immediate community, and persons who may later partake of other services this ministry will provide. The Dinah Project has often used excerpts from worship services as a starting point for discussion about sexual violence when conducting conferences or community education events. Excerpts from sermons and videotapes have also been used during group counseling to begin wrestling with some of the pertinent issues.

The only caution with recording the services is the need to protect the confidentiality of those who participate in the service. Invited preachers should be informed that they will be video- or audiotaped. It is a common courtesy to provide the preacher with a copy of the tapes that are made. Persons giving testimony or otherwise participating in the program should be informed that they are being taped. They may wish to use only a first name. The Dinah Project makes a practice of never recording the workshop that accompanies the theme of forgiveness. When there is a high level of audience participation, persons should not have to worry about speaking eloquently or where their statements may end up after the workshop.

Be prepared with audio and video services. If your church cannot do this in-house, consider asking a church member or professional to tape the services for you. At the very least, tape the sermon with a handheld tape recorder. This tape can continue to be an inspiration for the church and the wider community long after the event has ended.

DEVELOP A BUDGET

Each point in organizing the service will cost money. When constructing the budget for the worship event, remember administrative costs such as opening the church at a different time (if that is how the event has been scheduled), the cost of heating or cooling the building, and security (if necessary).

Consider the honorarium for the preacher and any expenses associated with bringing in a preacher from outside of the community: airfare, accommodations, and meals. A workshop leader may have particular needs for the presentation, such as copying, overhead projectors, or flip charts. Be sure to ask ahead of time and have those items available. Childcare, transportation, the reception, and recording all have associated costs. Publicity is low-cost, but there are costs associated with flyer design, copying, and postage. Don't forget to calculate the cost of printing the worship guides/bulletins.

There are a myriad of ways to finance a worship event. The church may be able to underwrite the expenses, or some agency or business may be willing to cosponsor the event. Worship services can be categorized as cultural or artistic events. Many corporations set aside money specifically for sponsoring cultural arts programs in local communities. Consider approaching local companies for these types of donations.

Before feeling overwhelmed at the unexpected costs of the worship service, remember that many of these services can be available at low or no cost.

UTILIZE VOLUNTEER ACTIVITY

Do not underestimate the power of volunteer activity in making a successful worship event. Many people in your congregation and in the community may feel excited about the work you are beginning to do, and they may ask about ways in which they can contribute. Many persons who are already working in the field of advocacy against sexual violence will happily provide services and expertise for little or no cost. There may be persons within your own church who have skills that can be utilized for the worship service preparation, for example, graphic designers or childcare workers. Other needed activities do not require any high level of expertise or skill—just a willingness to help. You can use volunteers from your church or community for the following types of activities:

- Faxing out press releases and delivering flyers and pictures
- Designing the flyer and worship guides/printed bulletin
- Follow-up calls to media and agency representatives
- Agency representatives available for aftercare or children's activities
- Childcare
- Video-/audiotaping
- Prayer partners for aftercare issues
- Catering or food preparation for the repast
- Distributing worship guides/printed programs during the event
- Serving as ushers during the events
- Providing transportation

Utilizing volunteer activity not only reduces the cost of the worship event, but it gives ownership of the event to the entire church community. By allowing for a wide level of participation, we practically reinforce the belief that sexual violence is a community issue and the community needs to be active in responding to it.

EVALUATE THE EVENT

It is always important to conduct an evaluation of each worship event. Whether the evaluation is formal or relatively informal, systematized evaluations allow the church to learn from and improve on each service, as well as to organize the documentation of each event. In the evaluation process, be sure to include the following:

- Get an estimate of the number of attendees.

- Maintain records of the event—publicity flyers, press releases, newspaper clippings, worship guides/printed program, audio- and videotapes.

- Follow up with those requesting information about services.

- Gather ministers, a random sampling of attendees, or an advisory committee to get their impressions. Ask these important questions: What went well? What could have gone better? What types of people seemed to be in attendance? How can we reach more people or a different population at the next service?

- Listen to the tapes of the service and record what you learned from statements given by participants or the invited preacher.

8

go tell it on the mountain:
community education

"Go tell it on the mountain, over the hills and everywhere."

T his Christmas carol invites us to tell everyone the good news of
Jesus' birth. Because we have experienced the joy of knowing
Jesus, we want everyone else to know about it. We want to write
it on the billboards and shout it from the mountaintops. Once I learned
more about sexual violence, I wanted to tell the whole world. I wanted
everyone else to know the statistics and the numbers. I wanted people to
know where to get help for themselves or their loved ones. I wanted people to understand how painful the experience of sexual violence can be.

Admittedly I was selfish. I wanted to create the world that I didn't find
when I was raped. I wanted to make a better world for future rape victims
than the one I encountered. I was a Dinah and I wanted people to hear
and notice me. The end result was the same: I wanted to tell everyone the
good news. The church can be a safe place once we all know more and
know what to do.

Community education may be the most important and transformative
part of a ministry that addresses sexual violence. Because there is so much

misinformation and lack of accurate information about the crisis of sexual violence, all educational efforts have an impact on those who are able to participate. Through educational efforts, church ministries can begin to equip clergy, laity, and social service workers to address the spiritual and theological crises that accompany the experience of sexual violence.

You don't have to be an expert on sexual violence to provide community education about it. You simply need to know the experts in your community and invite them to participate. This will often meet many of their own personal or organizational goals for outreach, while also keeping your congregation and faith community connected to those working in the field.

In almost every context of community education, there are four primary goals:

- To learn basic information about the crisis of sexual violence
- To begin to understand the experiences and consequences of sexual violence
- To critically examine the Scripture's contribution to the issue of sexual violence
- To learn some helpful ways to respond to the crisis of sexual violence

In her book *Violence in the Family: A Workshop Curriculum for Clergy and Other Helpers*, Marie Fortune provides one of the best resources in the field of Christian education regarding sexual abuse. In this book, Fortune addresses domestic violence against women and child sexual abuse. This sourcebook is divided into four parts. The first part gives the preparation for a church programmatic effort, including religious rationale for addressing these issues, goals and objectives, and educational methodology. The second part, entitled "application," gives details for ways to plan one- to two-day in-services that would provide training for clergy and other helpers. This part is incredibly helpful in terms of creative approaches to difficult issues and ways to discuss these topics in large or small group settings. The third part lists informational resources, such as fact sheets, available print and audiovisual resources and sample registration and evaluation forms. The last part is a series of articles for clergy addressing topics such as rural and urban settings, the role of forgiveness and justice-making, legal aspects of counseling and reporting, and family reconciliation.

I do not wish to duplicate Fortune's efforts and I highly recommend using her book as you begin working on community education. Fortune's workbook does, however, assume that community education is occurring in an in-service format with registered participants. The Dinah Project has found that most of its community education has happened on a much smaller level with small groups of clergy, college students, or vacation Bible school attendees. There have been time allotments of fifteen minutes to two hours in which to conduct the majority of community education efforts. Here, I share some of the forms and information that we have used.

Community education on sexual violence targets three types of audiences: (1) clergy, (2) laity and volunteers, and (3) social service and health workers. Each of these audiences presents different types of needs and comes with different bases of information. With clergy, the emphasis tends to focus on basic information about sexual violence and ways in which clergy can respond. Handouts with bibliographic information and the spiritual and theological impact can be used for covering that amount of information. With social service and health workers, on the other hand, you can usually assume that the audience already has more than basic knowledge about the crisis of sexual violence. With these participants, we linger on biblical passages that are problematic and those with hope, and the spiritual and theological impact of sexual violence. Laity and volunteers usually need the full gamut of information from "Sexual Violence 101" to biblical passages and ways to be responsive. This type of information can be given in small doses in Bible studies or church school. Laity and volunteers also have varying levels of interest in specific information. Some laypersons only want basic knowledge of the crisis and the faith perspectives on sexual violence. Others may want to know how they can respond effectively or be part of a prayer or follow-up team. For this reason, it is important to structure sexual violence education for laity and volunteers with rotating components where people can sit in on the informational sessions that most interest them and the type of volunteer work they will be giving to the ministry.

When conducting community education sessions, whether they are fifteen minutes in duration or a couple of hours, there are two basic items that must always be included.

- Always provide handouts
- Always give some time for a question-and-answer period

When providing handouts, there are five basic types of information that will be helpful to all audiences that are addressed:

- The goals and objectives of the session
- Church contact information—brochure or phone number and contact person
- Statistics on and definitions of sexual violence
- Popular effective and ineffective responses
- Bibliography

Providing this type of information in print will cut down on the time it takes for questions and answers, as well as serve as a ready reference for persons to look at in the future. When compiling handouts, you can also keep in mind that statistics may change every year or so, but these five items can be staples in the revolving handouts used for various settings.

Other aspects of community education are designed to (1) find out where people are, (2) engage the Christian tradition and, (3) introduce the spiritual issues surrounding sexual violence. As with the worship services, the more creative the presentation, the more memorable and easier it is to engage workshop participants.

FINDING OUT WHERE PEOPLE ARE

When there is only a small amount of time in which to educate, a quick questionnaire is a good way to get people involved. This is particularly effective with clergy and laity who may know little of the basic information about sexual violence. Participants can fill out the questionnaire as they take their seats or eat a meal before the presentation. A large part of the presentation can involve going over the questionnaire's correct answers and elaborating with the accurate information. Be careful about responding to questions. The questionnaire will often raise a couple questions from the audience for each item listed. In order to save time, be sure to ask people to hold their questions until the end because they may hear the answer during the presentation.

ENGAGING THE TRADITION

It is always important to look at what we have learned about sexual violence from the Christian tradition. Include both biblical sources and theological sources that influence the way many Christians think. This information can be provided in a printed list or in a more interactive format. The Dinah Project often prints scriptures that contain incidents of sexual violence, breaks the workshop participants into small groups, and gives participants questions to answer in regard to each passage. At the end of a fifteen-minute time period, each group can choose a spokesperson to give a two-minute summary of their passage and what they learned. This format works well for vacation Bible schools, church schools, or longer workshops. It also allows persons to read neglected sections of the Bible and examine their own ideas about God and sexual violence. Most importantly, they can continue the study at home when they have more time to look at the passages and reflect on their own impressions.

INTRODUCING THE SPIRITUAL ISSUES SURROUNDING SEXUAL VIOLENCE

This is the time to be creative and interactive. In situations where there are time constraints, these issues can be listed and given a couple quick points. This process has worked with brief time allotments working with social service providers. Nevertheless, the most effective ways of educating people involve the arts and audience participation.

This is a good time to use some of the creative elements from the worship service. The exercise "Layers" (see appendix D) can be used almost anywhere with a chair, seven white sheets, fourteen slips of paper, and fifteen audience volunteers. After the presentation, ask participants how they felt watching the dramatization. Ask the person sitting in the chair how it felt to be underneath the sheets. What do people learn about both the experience of sexual violence and the ways in which community leaders or friends can be helpful or discouraging?

Sometimes the actors from the skits are available outside of the worship experience and they can take their "show on the road." The Dinah Project used a skit to introduce social and spiritual issues of sexual violence and the three to four actors happily took fifteen minutes to perform the presentation. Again, workshop participants had a worksheet with questions whereon they could reflect on their responses to the presentation.

If you don't have traveling actors or sheets, feel free to use excerpts from recordings of worship services. Use parts of testimonies or the sermon. People can listen to or watch five minutes and talk about different elements that arose from one individual view of sexual violence. Some testimonies naturally lend themselves to a discussion of the theological issues and the healing process.

When providing more intensive and thorough lay and volunteer training, drawing upon community resources prevents reinventing the wheel. Invite individuals from local rape crisis centers and the therapeutic community in your local area to provide information on different aspects of sexual violence. Be sure to invite male and female speakers that represent different dimensions of the experience of sexual violence. Remember: some agencies provide their own volunteer training, and it may be more efficient to participate in the training offered by these agencies while only adding a couple sessions that talk about your particular church and the faith perspective.

In the longer training, cover such topics as your own church's structure and ministry and how this particular type of ministry fits into the overall theology and activity of the local congregation. It's also important to talk about the roles and responsibilities of volunteers: ethical issues, confidentiality, and similar issues. Learning about post-traumatic stress disorder and effective communication are other important aspects of volunteer training. These components may be applicable to other aspects of the church's ministry, so consider inviting those who work with children or other health issues as well.

When The Dinah Project plans intensive volunteer training, it covers subfields of sexual violence: nonoffending parents and loved ones, adult survivors of childhood sexual abuse, children who are violated, dealing with offenders, and same-gender versus different gender violation. Most importantly, include information about the spiritual and theological issues that arise from the context of sexual violence. In this longer session, there is no need to give all the answers. It is simply important to raise the issues and inform persons about the current state of things. At the end of the session, list different ways that people can volunteer with the ministry. The Dinah Project's volunteer opportunities span from faxing press releases to ushering at a worship service to cooking meals for therapy group to participating in the speakers' bureau. Be sure to include ways that volunteers and coordinators can record the amount of time that is donated to the ministry. Evaluate the training at the end. Again, consult Fortune's *Violence in the Family* for more concrete ideas.

SPEAKERS' BUREAU

One of the most critical and short-term ways to impact your community regarding the crisis of sexual violence is to develop a speakers' bureau. A speakers' bureau is a list of persons who are knowledgeable about the faith perspective on sexual violence and are willing to speak in public. The more your congregation is known for addressing this issue, the greater the request for speakers.

Volunteers who have undergone longer training can be excellent speakers. Perhaps there are survivors or former offenders who are willing to share their stories as well. Speakers can attend conferences, rallies, college campus events, or radio and television programs. Most events only take one to three hours of time on a rather infrequent basis. Be sure to provide care for speakers. Speaking to a large crowd or on a radio program can be very draining for the speaker. Speakers will benefit from volunteer buddies who provide transportation, accompany the speaker, give water or favorite foods, and listen attentively after the event is over.

EVALUATING THE EDUCATIONAL SESSIONS

It is always helpful to conduct an evaluation of each community education session. This may not be feasible for the speakers' bureau, but do ask for feedback from the host of the program. Anonymous evaluation forms will give vital input on ways in which training can be improved for future workshops. Evaluations also help to keep records of the number of attendees in each session. In the evaluation process, be sure to include the following:

- Get an estimate of the number of attendees.
- Maintain records of event—handouts, curricula.
- Follow up with those requesting information about services or with longer questions.
- On evaluation forms ask: Did you learn anything? Was the time well utilized? Is there additional information you would have liked to have had? What was the most effective lesson learned? What was the least stimulating activity? Would you recommend this training to others you know? If so, may we contact you?
- Listen to any tapes of the session and listen for ways in which the workshop can be improved. Note positive learning moments as well as places where the audience and speakers disconnected.

9

weep with those who weep: group counseling

I have always liked the passage in the book of Job when Job's friends realize what has happened to him. They come running to Job's house and they put on sackcloth and ashes and they sit with him. They mourn with Job. Before they start talking to Job they did exactly what I wanted and needed my friends to do—the only thing they could do, just sit with me and share my pain.

What Job needed and what I needed was community. We needed someone else around us. We needed to know that we were not alone. We needed to hear the voices of other people who have had the same experiences. We needed to hear the voices of people who believe that if we put our heads together, things will eventually be okay. Community is supposed to be about empathy. Generally we like to share our joys, our hopes, our dreams, and our successes. We are less apt to share our fears, our doubts, and our sorrows. But this is what most of us need the most. And this is what brings us out of our low periods and our funks. It is the presence of other caring people that transforms us.

Providing counseling to survivors is one of the most challenging and intimate aspects of a ministry that addresses sexual violence. It requires a great deal of time and commitment, but it also holds the potential for the ministry's most tangible transformation of the lives of individuals. This is the "sitting with our Dinahs." When offering counseling services, the ministry moves from addressing sexual violence through prevention and education to providing direct services to "clients."

The Dinah Project chooses to offer therapy groups rather than support groups. Therapy groups have licensed therapists as leaders, particular programs, and a set number of individuals in the group. Support groups tend to be peer-led and are open to new members at all times. A therapy group allows individuals to set particular goals for themselves and gives them a consistent setting in which to work towards these goals. Support groups, on the other hand, are fluid and people come as they feel a need for camaraderie or help with a particular issue.

You may automatically think: Well, there are therapists and rape crisis centers that provide counseling to people who have experienced sexual violence. Why should the church offer counseling? And why offer group counseling?

WHY THE CHURCH?

The church is uniquely positioned to provide a spiritual underpinning to a therapeutic session. It is unfair to fault therapists for a failure to address the faith crises that accompany the experience of sexual violence. Matters of faith are the expertise of the faith community. The church offers the hope of new life, the promise of resurrection after death, the healing power of Jesus Christ, a community of believers. The list goes on. While the church can help to educate agency workers about ways in which they can be more sensitive and responsive to faith issues in psychological counseling, the church can also provide a more integrated model of spiritual and psychological counseling.

The church is also uniquely positioned to break down many of the barriers that persons have in seeking out other types of counseling. For those persons who feel shame and embarrassment about their experiences, it can be very difficult to explain to one's friends or family that one will be out of the house for a couple hours to get therapy at the local rape crisis center. It is much easier to say, "I have a meeting at church." Other persons may reject traditional counseling because of its lack of spiritual emphasis. Some people feel as though traditional counselors do not understand the important faith perspective that they are bringing to their experience. This tension often arises around issues of forgiveness, sexuality, and suffering and evil.

In regards to the perceived and real stigma of seeking psychological counseling, The Dinah Project has found that the word "therapy" still frightens off many potential participants. For that reason, we named the group counseling component "Dinah Groups." We later explain to participants the difference between therapy and support and the type of direction we hope to provide.

WHY GROUP COUNSELING?

The Dinah Project is committed to group counseling because it emphasizes the community dimension of the impact of sexual violence. It can be argued that the worst part of the experience of rape, incest, or sexual assault is the feeling victims have that they are the only ones in the world who understand how they feel. Group settings quickly negate this feeling by giving individuals a chance to meet others who are struggling in similar ways. Members of the group can share their experiences of pain and triumph with each other and encourage each other. This model reflects the scriptures that encourage believers to empathize with each other and support each other in difficult times.

"Rejoice with those who do rejoice, and weep with those who weep" (Rom. 12:15).

"Without counsel, plans go wrong, but with many advisors they succeed" (Prov. 15:22).

When organizing the group counseling component of the ministry, the Dinah Group has focused on the following areas:

- Work with local agencies and universities
- Make good use of publicity
- Have small gender-separate groups
- Encourage individual counseling as well
- Establish a safe and comfortable place
- Document, document, document
- Remove barriers to participation
- Develop a format and topics
- Utilize volunteer activity
- Budget

WORK WITH LOCAL AGENCIES AND UNIVERSITIES

Do not feel as though you, as clergy, church worker, or laity, should possess the skills to conduct group counseling. Simply find the people who have the skills. Draw upon the strengths of various facets of the community and establish healthy collaborations. Perhaps the church already knows of a therapist or social worker willing to give time and resources to the groups. Perhaps the individual is a member of the congregation. If not, seek out those contacts in local agencies. Talk with the executive director or director of counseling services about having a staff therapist work with your groups. They may be able to include this in the staff member's salary or provide other incentives for volunteering time. They can also refer other people who work in the field who may be available or knowledgeable about available counselors.

Also look at local colleges, universities, or seminaries for students who need placements for internships. These students may already have a wealth of knowledge about sexual violence, group counseling techniques, or some of the ways to wrestle with theological dilemmas and spiritual crises. Because students are required to work in local agencies, they will often work free of charge or for very low rates.

Most importantly, experts in the area already know some of the techniques and methods of group counseling. They have experience with intakes, documentation, different methods of unearthing difficult issues, and so on. These are specialized skills that professional counselors constantly refine.

On the other hand, you do not want to leave the group counseling entirely to the therapeutic professional. Group counseling should be led by at least two persons. The second person should have knowledge, expertise, and comfort in talking about the spiritual and theological crises of sexual violence. This person should be familiar with the literature in the field and should consider training at the various national conferences. Designing the group counseling with multiple leaders also gives one leader the room to have a crisis or miss a meeting without having to cancel meetings.

These collaborations are wonderful ways to bridge some of the gaps that tend to exist among faith, therapeutic, and academic institutions. By bringing different people together to meet one common goal, group counseling efforts may be making radical network connections for their local areas.

MAKE GOOD USE OF PUBLICITY

As a new effort, the group counseling requires a lot of unique publicity. As with the worship services, basic community service announcements and press releases are helpful. Nevertheless, the sensitive issue of sexual violence requires some personal and unconventional methods as well.

Design flyers to get attention and provide ample information. Post these flyers in places where people feel comfortable writing down phone numbers—bathroom stalls and locker rooms. Post flyers around church and send flyers to other congregations. Announce the group counseling component whenever there is a worship event or community education session. Actively seek out participants from those desiring follow-up to worship events or community education. Talk to therapists at rape crisis centers or individual practices. Tell them about the proposed group and ask if they have any clients whom they believe could benefit from such a healing experience. Ask if you can make a brief presentation at an agency staff meeting or ministers' fellowship introducing and informing others about the group counseling that is available.

HAVE SMALL GENDER-SEPARATE GROUPS

Separating individuals based on gender is key to the success of group counseling. There tends to be a greater comfort level and ease to talk about the gender-specific issues that will arise during the sessions. The leaders of the group should also be of the same gender as the participants. The Dinah Group began with groups for women simply because there was a greater response from women requesting services. Men's groups require different language and marketing. Men's fellowships or breakfast groups can serve as group counseling sessions that deal with sexuality and power. Because sexual violence is still largely identified as a women's issue, many men are reluctant to participate in a group that is specifically about dealing with sexual violence. Nevertheless, men may congregate under different headings and accomplish some of the same goals and activities.

Keep groups small in number. Assume that two to three individuals will not stay for the entire program. Some individuals are not as committed as they originally believe they are. For some people, the pain of wrestling with these issues is too great for them. Do not chastise those who decide not to follow through with full participation. Continue to follow up with them on an individual basis, and remind them that they are welcome to attend the next program when they are ready. Other people truly desire to attend all sessions, but there are time conflicts. For this reason, the

Dinah Group changed evenings of the week for each twelve-week program. The Dinah Group found that three or four active participants easily utilized the time allotment for each session. With a small number, each individual has an opportunity to share and receive personalized attention within the group setting.

ENCOURAGE INDIVIDUAL COUNSELING

Many participants benefit from concurrent individual counseling with the group counseling. Perhaps your church has the resources from which to provide group and individual counseling. If not, many participants may want to investigate individual counseling through the local rape crisis center. Other participants may prefer to come to group counseling after completing individual counseling, and others may feel a need for individual counseling after the program has ended. Group counseling should not cancel out the benefits of the deeper exploration and attention that individual counseling can provide. Rather, it can enhance the experience of individual counseling.

ESTABLISH A SAFE AND COMFORTABLE PLACE

While the worship services and community education components strive to make the church a safe place for dealing with sexual violence, group counseling must be more than intentional in creating a safe and comfortable place for the emotional and spiritual excavation that is going to take place during sessions.

Ensure Confidentiality

Every participant should understand and be assured of confidentiality. Draft a statement of confidentiality that is signed by all participants, leaders, and volunteers. Participants should have the right to concealed identity and personal information. Let participants know the circumstances under which confidentiality must be breached—intent to harm self or others and reporting of child abuse. Also inform participants that they are not to share the stories of their coparticipants outside of the group setting. Trust is a major issue for many survivors of sexual violence. One of the best ways to help rebuild the ability to trust is by proving to be trustworthy. The facilitators must treat the stories and details of each participant like the pearls of great price that they are.

Also establish confidentiality within the church. Choose a time when no one else is scheduled for an activity at the church, or use a separate entrance from the main doors to the building. Although you will want to publicize the existence of the group, do *not* publicize the day and time to anyone who does not need to know. Caterers, security personnel, volunteers, and group participants are the only persons who need to know when the group meets. This helps people to feel as if their confidentiality is maintained outside of the group as well.

Closed Groups

After three weeks, close the group to any new participants. Doing this will allow the participants the opportunity to bond and feel safe and comfortable with each other. If there are new persons dropping in and out of the group, participants do not get the chance to develop the interpersonal relationships that help the environment to be collegial and secure. New persons coming in and out of the group also means that individuals may feel as if they have to retell their stories or update new people on the details of their lives so that a statement can be understood. If there are people who express interest in participating in the group after it has been closed, feel free to do an intake and indicate that the person may participate in the next session. In the meanwhile, suggest individual counseling through the church (if available), a private therapist, or a rape crisis center.

A Comfortable Setting

Try to provide the most comfortable setting possible. Rather than sitting in chairs or pews, use a smaller section of the church or a church office. Provide room to sit on chairs, couches, or floor pillows. Have stuffed animals or soft balls nearby. Many people prefer to hold onto something while engaging in this challenging work. Others like to doodle. Doodling does not indicate a lack of attention. It may help the person to focus. Have markers, journals, crayons, and large sheets of paper available for particular exercises and doodling.

DOCUMENT, DOCUMENT, DOCUMENT

Document all the work that is done in the group counseling sessions. This can be a delicate issue considering the constraints of maintaining confidentiality. When creating client files, inform participants that these are necessary for keeping records. Tell the clients what individuals have access to these files, and who does not. Ensure that the facilitators are the only individuals with access to the files. Keep them in a locked file cabinet in a locked room or closet. Do not use client names on the outside of the file folders. When writing in client files, indicate the topics discussed and the level of participation. There is no need to be incredibly specific about the details of each client. Should the files be subpoenaed for any reason (as when a client has a case that is undergoing legal proceedings), there will not be any information in the files that further injures the individual. The professional therapist will be able to provide additional guidance on this issue.

Also record the goals of each participant at the beginning of the program. A review of these goals at the end of the session will help individuals to see how much progress they have made. Some people will grow in the direction they had hoped. Others will have grown in ways they did not anticipate. A written record of these goals means more to the participant than to the program's documenting system.

Record the topics of each session. Some sessions have planned topics, while others flow freely from the interests and needs of the participants on a particular day. Recording the topics will give you an idea of ways to plan future sessions and help to identify the issues that seem to be the most pertinent for the population that is being served.

Record the time that is spent giving counseling. Create forms and procedures for noting the number of hours that therapists and spiritual counselors are giving to the group counseling components. If the facilitators feel comfortable in giving out a personal phone number for counseling outside of the group setting, they should record the time spent in conversation. This counts as time spent giving counseling.

Although recording may feel tedious, it is critical for assessing the time needed to coordinate the group counseling component. If a facilitator is being paid an hourly wage, documenting hours indicates the amount of money needed to run the program. When seeking support from granting sources, tight documentation will assist in obtaining federal or private dollars for coordinating the program. You will be able to give more detailed information on grant requests and indicate a history of strong documentation.

REMOVE BARRIERS TO PARTICIPATION—TRANSPORTATION, MEALS, CHILDCARE

Some of the primary barriers to participation in the group counseling can be met by eliminating them. A person should be able to participate if s/he has the time and the desire. Money, childcare needs, transportation, or hunger should not prevent individuals from receiving the services they need and want. If someone has made the decision to work on his/her deepest and most painful issues, there should be no further hurdles to jump.

Much like the barriers that keep people from attending worship services, four primary barriers to receiving group counseling are

- The cost of psychological counseling
- A need for child care
- Transportation
- Time conflicts with meal times

Psychological counseling can cost up to $150 per hour. This is an intimidating issue for many persons whether or not they have health insurance. Health insurance usually provides for individual counseling, but for only a certain number of hours per year from a limited list of clinicians. If the church can provide services free of charge, participants will not have to be concerned about the exhorbitant cost of counseling.

It has, however, been noted that people tend to place a greater value on those things for which they pay. Some persons seem to take advantage of free services by demonstrating low commitment or irregular attendance. The Dinah Project has asked participants to give something of their substance to the program or to the church. This donation can range from monetary gifts to clothes or toys for children's programs to canned food for the food bank or time to one of the church's ministries. This type of "payment" is more of a suggestion than a requirement, but there have been no problems with persons happily giving to the church. In fact, some participants of the group counseling go on to serve as speakers, worship service participants, or other volunteers for The Dinah Project.

Provide childcare or activities for children. You should provide a separate section for children during the group counseling. Find out the ages of the clients' children. If programs occur during the school year, teenagers from the church may be available to tutor younger children. Since parents are just a short distance away, professional childcare is usually not necessary. Nevertheless, parents should not have to worry about occupying children while they are trying to receive emotional and spiritual assistance.

Again, host the sessions during a time when transportation is available. Schedule sessions while bus or subway lines are still running to your building. Perhaps the church van is available to pick up persons who want to attend but cannot provide their own transportation. Perhaps volunteers can rally together to pick up or drop off clients. Have money available for taxis in case of unforeseen transportation needs. Some participants may want to carpool after they get to know each other better.

If sessions are held during a weekday evening or morning, be sure to provide a full meal. We have held Dinah Groups on the evenings of a weekday. Understand how difficult it may be for participants to get off work, pick up children from school or daycare, run home, and prepare a meal before attending. Let persons know that they can receive a full meal that will be healthy for them and their children. Allow half an hour of the meeting time for eating and fellowshipping over the meal. During the intake, learn the allergies and diets of the participants so that there is at least one dish that they can eat at each meal.

The Dinah Group meals consist of at least one protein selection (meat or soy), one vegetable dish, one starch (bread or potatoes), a beverage, and some type of dessert. For morning meals, provide a protein or warm dish along with fruit, starches (such as muffins, bagels) and a beverage.

DEVELOP A FORMAT AND TOPICS

Your clients will be best served, and your time most efficiently spent, if you have done adequate preparation to set up the structure of the program and define the issues that will be addressed.

Format

Before beginning the program, allow three to four weeks for scheduling intakes for each client. Give one hour for each intake. During intakes, clients can meet the facilitators in a one-on-one setting, fill out the paperwork, and learn about confidentiality and more details about the program. This is the time to ask participants their personal reasons and goals for themselves in this program. Responses on client forms can give facilitators ideas for topics to cover and the depth of each participant's situation. Gathering this type of information before the program starts will give facilitators time to consult with other experts or with agencies should more comprehensive care seem necessary for an individual client.

Because weekends can quickly fill up with children's activities, our Dinah Groups choose a weekday evening for the sessions. Scheduling sessions at 6:00–8:00 P.M. gives participants the time to get off work. Dinner takes place at 6:00–6:30 P.M. Request that persons arrive no later than 6:15, but do not turn people away from coming as soon as they can before 6:45. After 6:45 P.M., a late attendee may interrupt the space that is created in the sessions.

Dinah Groups begin each session with a meditative moment on a scripture, song, poem, or reading from a Christian thinker. Each participant is invited to share or journal his or her feelings about the meditation. The meditation is chosen as an encouragement or expression of the topic of the day. Participants may want to take turns bringing in a favorite meditation. Sometimes stretching or breathing exercises are used to open each session. Consider using guided imagery or meditative chants as well. This can help to reduce the tension that exists at the end of the day or that may accompany the mere idea of digging through challenging issues.

After the meditation, begin by checking in with each participant. How are you feeling? How was your day? Did anything happen in the past week that you would like to share with the group? Try not to spend too much time on this section because you can spend hours on check-ins if they are not easily monitored. Try to begin discussing the topic for the day by 7:00 P.M. at the latest.

Dinah Groups end each session with prayer or scripture and prayer. The facilitators or the participants are invited to offer a prayer that speaks to some of the issues that have been discussed during the group. Framing the sessions in prayer and meditation clearly establishes the spiritual context for the counseling. This structure also reiterates that the love of God is needed to overcome and to heal from the difficult situations in our lives.

Topics

Topics can be divided into those that are specifically "spiritual" or "theological" and those that are "clinical." It will not take long to see that the boundaries between these two categories are somewhat artificial. The same issues that present emotional and psychological responses have accompanying spiritual effects. Nevertheless, this group counseling should be intentional about addressing some of the spiritual topics that traditional counseling tends not to cover:

Topics can include, but are not limited to:

- Forgiveness
- Sexuality and body image
- Healing
- Suffering and evil

Use responses to intakes to determine other issues that should be covered. Dinah Groups always take time to explain PTSD or rape trauma syndrome so that clients know that their responses and behaviors may be typical of the experience of great trauma. Other topics Dinah Groups have covered include:

- Anger
- Relationships with family members
- Romantic relationships
- Ways to relieve stress

Dinah Groups try to incorporate interactive programming as well. Use butcher paper for body drawings when discussing body image (I eventually found the paper in a teacher-supply store). Topics of forgiveness and sexuality tend to have formats similar to Bible studies. Bring in a guest speaker or expert to describe and teach different ways to relieve stress.

Also include time for the following basics of group counseling:

- Testimony
- Evaluation

Participants should have the opportunity to tell the story of their abuse. This is a very challenging task since the retelling may often feel like reliving. But the retelling is also empowering towards greater steps of healing. Naming the abuse for what it is can be a major milestone for a participant. Testimony is also an important part of the Christian tradition, wherein believers are known to share their experiences of trial and the ways in which they feel God is acting in their situations.

Participants should have the opportunity to evaluate their own progress and that of the program. Self-evaluations can be given as creative homework assignments. Dinah Groups have used "letters to the abuser" (not necessarily to be sent) or "lessons I've learned" statements or poems as means of helping participants to see the progress they have made by the last session. An anonymous evaluation form about the strengths and weaknesses of the program also helps to make future programs stronger and more focused.

UTILIZE VOLUNTEER ACTIVITY

Group counseling provides many opportunities for volunteers to participate in the ministry. Be sure that each volunteer understands the importance of confidentiality regarding the time, day, place, and identity of the members. Although the groups are separated by gender, the volunteers do not need to be specific to the gender of the groups. Dinah Groups have used volunteers for:

- Facilitators
- Meal preparation and clean-up
- Transportation
- Security—especially when sessions occur at night
- Childcare
- Donations of floor pillows, stuffed animals, soft balls, etc.

BUDGET

It is clear than such a large program requires a larger budget than other components of the ministry. Again, do not feel as if eighty thousand dollars is needed to run this component of the ministry. The generosity of volunteers has supported Dinah Groups when other funds were difficult to obtain. Try not to let the lack of money stop the ministry from providing services.

When budgeting, be sure to account for the following items. The church may already possess some of these items. Facilitators may be willing to donate their times or reduce their usual rate. Many items can go on a wish list distributed to church members, corporations or the larger community.

- **Therapist and spiritual counselor.** Count hours: Intakes (one hour times seven clients), travel time (a half hour times nineteen sessions and intakes), preparing for each session (one hour times twelve sessions), session time (two hours times twelve), recording on charts after session (one times twelve), phone counseling (six hours times twelve) equals 136.5 hours for each twelve-week program.

- **Publicity.** Count the cost of flyer design, copying, and postage.

- **Supplies for sessions.** Costs include copying for any handouts and purchasing (or having donated) journals, sketch pads, markers, crayons, clay, butcher paper, a flip chart, couches, pillows, floor pillows, beanbag chairs, stuffed animals, and soft balls.

- **Childcare.** Again, count hours. Intakes (one hour times seven clients) times sessions (two sessions at twelve weeks each) equals 31 hours.

- **Meal Preparation.** If catered, consider ten dollars per person for fifteen people (don't forget the children) times twelve weeks, which equals $1800. If donated by volunteers, offer to underwrite by fifty to sixty dollars per meal.

- **Security.** If meetings are held in the evenings or after sunset, security may help persons to feel safer when they enter or leave the building.
- **Administrative costs.** Remember the cost of heating or cooling the facilities, keeping the lights turned on, and related costs.

The decision to offer group counseling is no simple one. It involves a great deal of work that requires specialized expertise. On the other hand, you don't have to be a licensed therapist to incorporate counseling into your church's response to sexual violence. You do need good contacts and good organizational skills. At the beginning and end of the day, what you really need is the compassion to weep with those who weep, knowing that you will soon be rejoicing with those same people.

THREE TOUGH TOPICS

Three of the most recurring and difficult topics to address when examining the spiritual impact of sexual violence are:

- Sexuality
- Suffering and evil
- Forgiveness

Neither scholars nor church denominations nor local congregations nor an individual family unit have come to agreement on ways to address some of these ageless questions that impact our everyday spiritual lives. The Dinah Project does not attempt to provide definitive answers to these controversial topics. It is, however, important to wrestle with these topics and provide some direction in which to guide those who have undergone the experience of sexual violence.

The following three chapters discuss some of the ways in which the experience of sexual violence creates crises for its victims and the communities regarding issues of sexuality, suffering, and forgiveness. The Dinah Project suggests images that can be helpful in reconstructing the ways that we all grapple with these issues.

10

it's my body and i'll cry if i want to: *images of body and sexuality*

I used to like my body. I was trim and fit and young enough to show it off in short skirts, high heels, sleeveless tops, form-fitting dresses, hip-hugging bellbottoms, and halter-tops. I never felt threatened or inappropriate. I felt young and free.

I didn't know what to do with my body after I was raped. I wanted to be clean so I took several long showers. I wore baggy clothes because I didn't want to draw attention to my body. I considered sexual behavior that had never previously entered my mind. I wanted to feel like my body belonged to me again, like I had control over what happened to it. And yet I was convinced that it did not. It took years to figure out how to relate to my body again. I did some things right and I made some mistakes. Over time, I learned to dress appropriately, love myself, and make intelligent decisions about who did and did not have access to my body. The memory of the rape no longer colors my decisions about physical or sexual intimacy. But I've never again felt like I was completely safe from someone else's stronger or more powerful attack on my body. I still reserve the right to cry over that loss.

People who experience sexual violence experience a profound separation from their body, indeed, from their entire selves. The nature of sexual violence is an invasion of the body. Yet it also affects the spirit, the self. The sense of integration and control between self and body is fragmented in the trauma. Some aspects of the Christian tradition assert that a body can be violated, while the spirit is left intact. This type of spirit-body separation is particularly destructive for victims of sexual violence because their reality contradicts this philosophy. The Dinah Project stresses the unity of the body and the spirit to begin to reconstruct images of the body and sexuality.

WHAT IT FEELS LIKE: CONNECTED AND FRAGMENTED AT THE SAME TIME

By its very definition, sexual violence is an assault on the body. But sexual violence is not the same as a punch on the arm or a slap in the face. To be violated sexually is to be assaulted in the most vulnerable region of a person's being—the sexual self. The assault is humiliating and degrading. Sexual violence not only assaults, it dominates. In acts of sexual violence, an individual is overpowered and invaded. The body is injured, but so is the soul, the person's sense of self, the individual's feelings about the self and body. Sexual violence separates the body from the spirit. In other words, sexual violence violates the spiritual self along with the body.

On the one hand, it seems strange to assert that the body is violated and the spirit is not. The body and spirit are united together and violated together. On the other hand, the normal sense of integration between body and spirit is corrupted in PTSD. PTSD destroys the integrated sense of self and the control over the body. PTSD also begins a painful dialectic of intrusion and constriction as the victim tries to cope with the overwhelming threat of fear and danger.

Persons with PTSD often experience flashbacks, nightmares, insomnia, and other psychosomatic responses to the trauma of the sexual violence (see the description of PTSD in chapter 4). A victim of sexual violence often loses control over when, where, and how a flashback may occur. Anything from a particular smell to the sight of the violator may cause the victim to relive the trauma, invoking a very real bodily response. In these situations, the victim has lost that normal sense of control over the body and its functions. No matter how much one may will it or desire it, the body is doing its own thing, reacting, freezing, remembering. The mind and spirit cannot control it. The normal unity of the body and spirit is destroyed.

This feeling gets worse. Not only does the violence cause a loss of body-spirit unity, but it does so in a disturbing dialectic between the overwhelming awareness of the violence and an emotional detachment from the same violence.

In the process of intrusion, victims are unable to control the way in which the memory of the violence affects them. The victim is always on guard for the threat of danger. "The average person" walks through life with the calm knowledge that anything *can* happen at any time to anybody. For the victims of PTSD, each moment feels as though it literally could be their last. Herman describes the feeling in this way:

> They [sufferers of PTSD] do not have a normal "baseline" level of alert but relaxed attention. Instead, they have an elevated baseline of arousal: their bodies are always on the alert for danger. They also have an extreme startle response to unexpected stimuli, as well as an intense reaction to specific stimuli associated with the traumatic event. . . . The traumatic events appear to recondition the human nervous system.[1]

The physical system within the human body is altered because the violation and the assault on the body continue long after the "actual crime" has occurred.

On the other hand, many victims experience "constriction." In this phase of the disorder, the victim loses an emotional connection to the bodily assault. For many victims, this process is one of dissociation whereby the spirit seems to actually leave the body and watch from a distant locale. Many survivors of sexual violence describe the experience of the violation as something they seemed to be watching from outside of themselves. It may be described as feeling like floating or hovering above one's own body. A victim can become detached from his or her own body, deadening the pain she or he might normally feel.

Many victims of sexual violence automatically constrict. For many people, constriction is the only coping mechanism available in the face of a horror too great for the consciousness to handle. Although it separates the spirit and body, constriction can also be seen as a gift. It protects an individual from otherwise unbearable pain and trauma. Constriction allows the victim to live *through* the trauma. It prevents the victim from pain that is greater than the psyche is prepared to handle. Although, this must be a *temporary* survival strategy, it can continue for years after the violation has ended.

For many victims of sexual violence, the two responses of intrusion and constriction go back and forth. This "dialectic" of opposing states is a characteristic feature of PTSD. This rhythm is a subconscious attempt on behalf of victims to reestablish control and balance in their lives. Herman states that altering between these two extreme states might be understood as an attempt to find a satisfactory balance. But balance is precisely what survivors lack.[2]

The dialectic of trauma is self-perpetuating. For this reason, many victims become strangers to themselves as well as to those around them. Victims may feel as though they no longer know themselves, or how they will feel or react in any setting. The violence has affected every aspect of the self.

Loss of Self

The experience of sexual violence also alienates individuals from themselves. That is, the sense of self is shattered by the trauma of sexual violence. Victims lose trust in themselves, other people, and God. Their self-esteems suffer from feelings of humiliation, guilt, and helplessness. The ability to be intimate is impaired by feelings of need and fear: The identity formed prior to the trauma is irrevocably destroyed. One survivor of sexual violence describes her experience of PTSD in this manner: "There's no way to describe what was going on inside me. I was losing control and I'd never been so terrified and helpless in my life. I felt as if my whole world had been kicked out from under me and I had been left to drift all alone in the darkness . . . I was convinced I was going crazy, and I'm still convinced I almost did."[3]

Difficulty with Future Sexual Relations

Because the sexual self is violated in the assault, the sexualities of those who have been sexually violated are dramatically affected. In *I Never Called It Rape*, Robin Warshaw describes the long- and short-term effects of sexual violence on sexuality: "Many victims experience sexual difficulties caused by physical injuries or emotional worries about their partners' reactions. They suffer a range of sex-related problems—the inability to relax, diminished arousal, sexual disinterest, or discomfort."[4] These symptoms may last for as little as a few days or as long as several years.

Nearly all victims of sexual violence experience difficulty reestablishing a healthy relationship to their sexualities. Some victims will not go out with persons who have some of the same physical characteristics as their assailants. Some people choose to be celibate after the trauma because of a fear of sexual intimacy. Others choose sexual promiscuity. One woman writes: "After I'd been raped, that changed; I just didn't care, my values changed. My mum always said to me, 'You shouldn't sleep with a man unless you love him.' But now that didn't count, I was sleeping with anyone. I think it was also that I was afraid to say 'no' to any man in case it led to violence again."[5] There is a reactionary response to one's own sexuality that lacks the unity intended between sexuality and spirit.

WHAT WE HAVE BEEN TAUGHT: THE SPIRIT IS MORE IMPORTANT THAN THE BODY

Churches must do all within their power to undermine thinking that supports a split between the body and the spirit. In the experience of sexual violence, the victim-survivor has become painfully aware of the connection between body and spirit. As the body is violated, so is the rest of the victim's self. On the other hand, the victim has difficulty reintegrating the body and the spirit. For both the victim and the assailant, a healthy relationship with one's own sexuality and the sexuality of others has been debased. One way in which to liberate the victim, the violator, and many others from this alienation is to promote religious teaching that unites the spirit and the body.

The Body-Spirit Split

Our Christian tradition contains elements that support a split between the spirit and body, as well as support for stressing spirit-body unity. Although most of Jesus' words and actions are those of unity and love, some statements support the separation of body and spirit. In Luke 12:4–5, Jesus says, "I tell you, my friends, do not fear those who kill the body, and after that can do nothing more. But I will warn you whom to fear: fear him who, after he has killed, has authority to cast into hell." This verse does not acknowledge the lived experience of many victims of sexual violence—that destroying the body also destroys the soul.

Paul is ambivalent about the connection between the spirit and the body. At times, he asserts spirit-body unity. In 1 Corinthians. 6:12–20, Paul writes about the connection between the human spirit and body. Other times, Paul's preference for the single state and his interpretation of marriage as human weakness (1 Cor. 7) indicates that the body and sexuality have a lower status than a life devoted to God. In addition, Christian ascetic and monastic traditions support the belief that the immortal spirit is temporarily imprisoned in a mortal body and spiritual elevation is sought through the subjugation, denial, and, at times, mutilation of the body.

On the other hand, there lies within Christian and biblical traditions a source of hope against the split of the body and spirit. Asserting the unity of the body and spirit means tapping into these aspects of the Christian traditions and wrestling with and teaching them.

ANOTHER VIEW: MY SPIRIT IS IN A BODY SO I'VE GOT TO DEAL

The Dinah Project discusses sexuality and body image through an investigation of particular scriptures, illumination of key points, and a series of questions designed to help individuals begin to think about ways to relate their faith and their sexualities.

It is important to know people's own ideas about sex and sexuality before even dealing with the Bible and Christian traditions. In Dinah Project counseling groups, we have used a large white board and brainstormed on the following topics:

- Participants' own definitions of "sex" and "sexuality"
- Ways in which participants express their sexuality.

This is a lighthearted and easy way to provide a safe place for discussing all the different things the members of the group bring to their own ideas about sex and sexuality. The second question has always made for a fun discussion of all the ways sexuality is expressed. We have received answers ranging from "short skirts" and "heels" to "dangling earrings," "my favorite cologne," or "the way I walk."

There are three scriptures on which The Dinah Project focuses for its teaching about sex and sexuality—Genesis 1:1–2:4a, 1 Corinthians 6:12–20, and Song of Songs/Song of Solomon.

GOD'S GIFT OF SEXUALITY
Genesis 1:1–2:4a (emphasis on verses 27, 31a)

The Genesis stories give us conflicting messages about men, women, their roles, and their sexuality. When we think of creation, we usually think of the Genesis 2:4b–3:24 narrative wherein God makes man from dust, breathes life into him, creates woman from man's rib, and the ensuing tale of the serpent, fruit, and what we have come to know as "the Fall." But there is another story that also gives a clue about human sexuality in the divine-human relationship. The creation story in Genesis 1:1–2:4a is one in which God speaks creation into existence.

Plot

God speaks into a formless void and forms the heavens, earth, and the rest of creation in sequence, while concluding at the end of each day that the creation is "good." On the sixth day, God creates both animals and humankind. Humanity is like the created animals in that they are both commanded to be fruitful and multiply and to eat of the same food. On the other hand, humans are distinct from animals in that they have dominion over the rest of the created order. There is no breakdown of species for humans; still they are the only part of creation that is gender-designated. The implication is that all of creation procreates, but only humans have sexuality. Humans are made in the image of God.

Lessons

- We are created in God's image.
- We are created sexual beings.
- Our sexualities are good. God created our sexualities and saw that it was "good."
- Men and women are created equally and are not opposite but rather harmonious sexes. Sexual differentiation does not mean hierarchy but rather equality. Created simultaneously, male and female are not superior and subordinate. Neither has power over the other; in fact, both are given equal power. Throughout this section, then, male and female are treated equally. Both man and woman are present and both have equal power over the earth. At the same time, neither is given dominion over the other.

What This Really Means

We have always been sexual beings. We do not become sexual beings at puberty. We tend to act as though children are asexual. However, careful observation reminds us that children are nurtured by a range of sensual experiences (hugging, kissing, and touching) that allow them to develop positive attitudes toward their bodies and themselves as sexual beings.[6] Child sexual abuse itself reminds us that children have sexualities that can also be manipulated and affected negatively.

The fact that we are created in God's image should remind us that there is something divine in everyone. The structure of humanity—including our sexuality—is acceptable and pleasing to God. Sexuality is a gift from God. It is not a curse or a burden. "Sex" and "sexuality" are not bad words or "its." We must feel free to know about the ways in which our bodies work. There is nothing shameful about how women wear bras and men sometimes wear jock straps; that women have menstrual cycles and men have genital erections. These are all biological functions of the human body. There should be no fear in understanding or exploring the body.

Also, we should not evaluate men and women differently. A sexually promiscuous woman is called a "'ho," "tease," or "skeezer." Promiscuous men are called "macks" or "players." Even dogs. What is the difference? We need to eliminate the double standard for men's and women's roles. Sexual control, for example, does not rest solely with the woman. It is not solely her responsibility not to dress provocatively and say "no." Likewise, the man need not always be the aggressor in relationships. Women can ask men out on dates, for example.

SEXUAL AND SPIRITUAL WHOLENESS: BODILY INTEGRITY
1 Corinthians 6:12–20 (emphasis on verses 19, 20)

I once heard a story about the flesh and the spirit. A student asks how to deal with the battle between the flesh and the spirit. On the one hand, "the spirit is willing and the flesh is weak" (Matt. 26:41) and Galatians 5:16–17 reads, "Live by the Spirit, I say, and do not gratify the desires of the flesh. For what the flesh desires is opposed to the Spirit, and what the Spirit desires is opposed to the flesh; for these are opposed to each other, to prevent you from doing what you want." In Romans 8:5–7, Paul writes that to be spiritually minded is life and to be carnally minded is death.

The students says, "We seem to have a constant conflict between being in the world and yet not of it, between being both spiritual and embodied. If these two parts of us are constantly warring against each other, who wins?"

The teacher replies: "Imagine two Dobermans of equal size and power who are constantly going at each other. They are each trying to kill the other, so that they can survive."

The student asks, "Which one wins?"

The teacher replies, "The one that you feed."

The teacher's message is that there are these two aspects of the self that are always in conflict—the body and the spirit—and the best way to ensure that the spirit wins is to "feed your spirit." The teacher encourages the students to control or limit the negative media influences that promote sexual promiscuity and the like, and to focus on Christian fellowship, the development and cultivation of purity and holiness.

The teacher's example is demonstrative of a split between the body and spirit. At times, it really does seem that the body and spirit *are* two separate warring entities. On the other hand, one knows that watching certain types of movies or videos or peers dressed in a certain way and the thoughts associated therein can cause the physical body to be aroused. Experience reminds us that there is clearly a connection between the inner person and the body.

In other portions of Scripture, Paul rejects this separation of body and spirit. In a passage often quoted for its edict to "flee fornication," Paul encourages Christians to be aware of the connection between the spirit and the body (1 Cor. 6:18–19).

Plot

In this letter to the church at Corinth, Paul writes to the Corinthians concerning questions of human leadership, sources of spiritual knowledge, spiritual gifts, the Eucharist, and the rapture. In a broader sense, Paul is trying to clarify the position of the Christian community within a wider secular world. In this section, Paul is addressing the practice of sexual immorality within the Christian community at Corinth. In chapter 5, Paul states with a tone of disdain that some Corinthians are engaging in sexual immorality — specifically the sexual relations between a man and his father's wife — without any shame (see 1 Cor. 5:1–3). This act may be a carryover from Greek and Roman cultures, which possessed a very free and liberal (anything goes) sexual ethic; nevertheless, Paul considers these acts evil. The problem, according to Paul, is that the Corinthians (the men) are engaging in these acts without shame or a sense of sin and repentance. Paul is disgusted because there is no communal judgment on this practice (1 Cor. 5:1–2).

Speaking to the Christian community, Paul reminds the Christians that they have been "washed and sanctified." Their status as "washed and sanctified" leads into the discourse in verses 12–20, because it reinforces the concepts that the Corinthian church must not conduct itself in the same manner as their non-Christian counterparts, and that there are consequences of being Christian. When writing of "fornication," it is unclear whether Paul is referring to practices of adultery, temple prostitution, or premarital sex in general. In this section, Paul makes these statements about the body in relationship to God:

- The body is meant for the Lord
- The Lord is meant for the body, as well
- Our bodies are members of Christ
- Sex (the physical act) unites people together (in a spiritual way)
- Christians are one with the Lord (in a spiritual way)
- Fornicators sin against their own bodies
- The Christian's body is the temple of the Holy Spirit
- God owns the body (there is a physical connection with God as well)
- Christians should glorify God in their bodies

Lessons

- The spiritual and physical aspects should not be separated
- Sexual relations create spiritual unity with one's partner
- The body belongs to God
- The body is a temple of the Holy Spirit
- We should glorify God in our bodies

What This Really Means

The spirit and the body need not be in conflict at all times. Knowing that our bodies belong to God and are holy temples, or dwelling places of God, means that we ought to respect our bodies. There are three ways in which we can respect our bodies:

God-respect: It is not only possible, but expected, that we worship God in our bodies. Dramatic sign language and liturgical dancing are examples of worshipping God in the body. There is not a great separation between what we consider to be spiritual acts of worship and how we operate in the physical body. Just as physical acts can be part of our spiritual relationship with God, so prayer and Bible study can be a part of our romantic relationships. When we see our bodies and the bodies of others, we must remember that they are dwelling places of the Holy Spirit—not just flesh and bones. What we do with the body is something we are doing with the body of God. We represent Christ in the actions we perform with our body.

Self-respect: Our bodies are beautiful to God in whatever form they are—in skin color, hair texture, physical stature. In God's eyes, we are not too short, too tall, too dark, too light, with good or bad hair, nose too broad or too thin, eyes too light or too dark. To God, it is all good. We can find our value in God, not in what the media or other people believe is beautiful or sexy. Respecting our bodies as temples of the Holy Spirit means that we respect these bodies ourselves. It also means that we are partially responsible for the upkeep of the temple. We should not be infiltrating our bodies with junk food or addictive substances. We ought to eat nutritionally and work out on a regular basis. The health of the physical temple is important to God.

Other-respect: Just as we respect our own bodies, we must respect the bodies of other people, and command this respect from others. This extends from rejecting the abusive treatment of our bodies by sexual or physical abuse from others, to resisting objectification of the body. We should not manipulate our bodies for the purpose of acceptance by others or conquest of another person. Although we interact in this world as embodied beings, we are more than bodies—we are spirits within the body. Some types of comments about our bodies, gestures toward our bodies, or bodily touches are offensive to us. We must make others aware of that and insist that they respect our body space.

RESPECT IN RELATIONSHIPS

Song of Solomon

On the one hand, the Hebrew Bible is filled with terrible images of male-female relationships. The first rapes in the Bible occurs in Genesis. There are several portrayals of relationships that are oppressive and demeaning to women—the rape of Tamar; the way in which Lot offers his daughters to the violent crowd in Sodom; the betrothal of women to men despite their love interest (Rachel, Leah, and Jacob); double standards about the punishment of adulterous men and women (Lev. 22)—to name a few. On the other hand, there is a story of mutual erotic love also found within the Bible:

> A garden locked is my sister, my bride,
> a garden locked, a fountain sealed (Song 4:12).

> Awake O north wind,
> and come, O south wind!
> Blow upon my garden,
> let its fragrance be wafted abroad.
> Let my lover come to his garden,
> and eat its choicest fruits (Song 4:16).

I come to my garden, my sister, my bride (Song 5:1a)

My beloved has gone down to his garden,
to the beds of spices,
to pasture his flocks in the gardens,
and to gather lilies (Song 6:2).

O you who dwell in the gardens,
my companions are listening for your voice;
let me hear it (Song 8:13).

Plot

Song of Solomon has been variously classified over the years as drama, poetry, love songs, wedding ritual liturgy, and erotic literature. It can best be described as a collection of poems that detail the relationship of two lovers and their quest for intimacy in a culture that does not readily accept their relationship.[7]

Its erotic content has caused many generations of scholars and Christians to question its inclusion in the Bible. It has traditionally been ascribed to King Solomon, although there is no indication that King Solomon wrote the book, and some even suppose that it was written by a woman during the Solomonic reign—perhaps one of his wives.[8] In attempts to understand why this type of literature is part of the Bible, scholars have offered various interpretations:

Allegory: This type of interpretation reads the literal sexual relationship between the two lovers as symbolic of God's mystical love for Israel, where Israel was God's bride. Christians have read the language as a celebration of the love of Christ, the bridegroom, for the Church, the bride.

Marital relations: As scholars and readers have come to take Song of Solomon more literally as erotic poetry, they attribute the sexual language and imagery to the marital relationship. They say that this exchange is the dialogue of a married couple extolling the beauty of married love.

Lessons

Passionate love is God-given (Song 8:6):
Set me as a seal upon your heart,
as a seal upon your arm;
for love is strong as death,
passion fierce as the grave.
Its flashes are flashes of fire, [also translated as "flames of the Lord"]
a raging flame.

Countering notions of beauty standards. There is appreciation for the human body without shame: "I am black and beautiful" (Song 1:5a). Whether the woman is "black" because of ethnic differentiation or because of class differentiation from working in the fields, it is clear that she believes that society does not consider her darker color to be beautiful. The breasts that the brothers of the female lover call small (Song 8:8: "We have a little sister, and she has no breasts"), the male lover describes thusly: "Your two breasts are like two fawns, twins of a gazelle" (Song 4:5a and 7:3)

The male lover is also described as sexually attractive (Song 5:11–15). Despite societal standards of beauty and sexuality, the two lovers find each other physically and sexually attractive. Together they conclude, as in the words of the king, that they are beautiful, "You are altogether beautiful, my love; there is no flaw in you" (Song 4:7).

Love in spite of cultural norms. One scholar notes that the Song of Solomon demonstrates love in spite of cultural norms. There is the call to the daughters of Jerusalem, "I adjure you, . . . do not stir up or awaken love until it is ready!" (2:7, 3:5, 8:4), the insistence that the lovers belong to each other (2:16, 6:3, 7:10), and the quick departures and hasty escapes (5:6–8, 8:14). This writer states that these passages indicate that "society, for inscrutable reasons, sought to keep [them] apart, perhaps because they were from different classes, from different ethnic backgrounds, or of a different color," nevertheless the Song indicates that they insisted upon togetherness despite these societal proscriptions on love.[9]

Mutuality and equality of power. Whereas Genesis 3:16 states that the woman's desire shall be for her man and he shall rule over her, Song of Solomon 7:10 indicates that there is mutual attraction: "I'm my beloved's and his desire is for me."

Interdependence and intimacy. The lovers are not just lusting partners: they have a level of intimacy that underlies their sexual relationship. Song of Solomon 5:16b states, "This is my beloved and this is my friend." The woman refers to her lover as "him whom [her] soul loves" (Song 3:1b).

Consideration of the pleasure of the other. The expression of mutual desire indicates that the partners are concerned about the pleasure of the other, as well as his/her own pleasure. This lesson is not applicable only in sexual relations, but also in terms of care and consideration in friendships and all levels of the romantic relationship.

Fidelity. The repeated refrain, variously stated, of "I am my beloved and he is mine" indicates faithfulness between the two lovers. They are committed to each other. They are concerned only with the other person, not the presence of others who find the lover attractive (5:9, 3:6–11). They do not identify ownership of the other's body, but refer to the other's body as "mine." There is never a sense of possessiveness, but a dedication to each other.

What This Really Means

Relationships should be mutual with consent in every arena of sexual and emotional intimacy. Sexual relations are not about treating another person as a trophy or conquest. Sexual relations should not be about popularity, pride, or ego. Rather the concern in a relationship is for the well-being of the other person, and the relationship is undergirded by friendship and love. There is acceptance and appreciation for the other person.

The Song of Solomon encourages us to value the other person in the relationship and to cultivate the relationship. The mutuality and fidelity in the relationship between the two lovers shows us an example of the type of respect for which we ought to strive. The fact that they were committed to the relationship and its maintenance despite societal expectations reminds us that love can transgress social categories of ethnicity and class.

Examining these scriptures does not solve the challenge of reconstructing sexuality after the experience of sexual violence. It does not end the flashbacks, nor can it restore the sense of safety or ownership. For these experiences, victims of sexual violence have the right to mourn and cry and holler until they can weep no more.

In the midst of the awkward feelings towards the body, the church needs to validate the spirit violation that occurs in sexual assault. We must encourage a reunion of the disintegrated body and self along with an ethic that respects one's own body and the bodies of others. We must assert that violence to the body is violence to the spirit. Investigation into different scriptures and individual and collective experiences with relationships and sexuality gives some footpaths to reconstructing body image and sexuality for survivors of sexual violence.

11

why didn't god stop it?
suffering and evil

When I was being raped, I prayed that God would stop it. I wanted God to intervene—lightning, a burning bush, something. I assumed that if God could part the Red Sea for the Israelites, then God could stop this one man from what he was about to do to me. But God did not. There was no mystical parting of the sea. No bushes burned. No lightning struck. And as far as I was concerned, God abandoned me when I needed God the most.

"Why didn't God stop it?" When I dared to voice my question, the answers I received hurt me even more than not having an answer at all. "The rape was a result of your own lack of faith." "God does not save those who enter into sinful or hazardous situations." "God had you go through this so you could learn something and help other people." None of these answers held much sway with me. They only made me feel worse. What kind of God, I wondered, could authorize this much pain in my life? I would rather someone had come out and said what I now say: "I don't know." I don't know why there is suffering and evil in the world. I don't know why

God seems to intervene at some times and not others. I don't know why God didn't stop it. I just don't know.

The experience of sexual violence inevitably forces the question: If God is all-good and all-powerful, then why is there suffering? This is a question that only churches can address. We need to cease providing easy answers to this question and begin to wrestle with different responses. Regardless of the response itself, as a church we must emphasize the overwhelming presence and compassion of God in the midst of the suffering of sexual violence.

WHAT IT FEELS LIKE: GOD HAS FORSAKEN ME

"I wasn't mad at God. I just had nothing to say to God." I repeated these words to my friends over and over again.

One of the most explicitly religious responses to sexual violence is a sense of abandonment by God. For someone in the religious community, the sense of trust in God is also affected. There is often a sense of distance from God in the midst of the profound suffering of sexual violence. There is a loss of trust in God's presence and goodness. Those affected by violence want to know:

- Where was God in the midst of the assault?
- Why didn't God stop the assault?
- Where is God now in the suffering of the healing process?
- If God is all-good and all-powerful, why is there suffering?

Even as a psychologist, Judith Lewis Herman identifies this type of questioning when describing PTSD:

> Survivors of atrocity of every age and every culture come to a point in their testimony where all questions are reduced to one, spoken more in bewilderment than in outrage: Why? The answer is beyond human understanding. Beyond this unfathomable question, the survivor confronts another, equally incomprehensible questions: Why me?[1]

Although a psychologist can note the problem of understanding suffering, for the Christian community, the question is specifically theological. Most of us believe that God is omnipotent, loving, and rewarding of righteousness. We then assume that suffering indicates God's displeasure with us. Most of us believe that God's presence protects us from suffering. But here we are suffering. Somehow we are outside of the presence of God. But then we believe that God is omnipresent. What does all this mean? What we think about God before we suffer largely determines the way in which we respond to the question of suffering.

WHAT WE HAVE BEEN TAUGHT: GOD LET IT HAPPEN (FOR A REASON)

Most of us have been taught that God is omnipotent, omnipresent, and omniscient—all-powerful, in all places at all times, and all-knowing. Let's look at omnipotence first. According to some theologians, the belief in a perfect omnipotent God leads to a sense of abandonment by God. The logic follows this pattern:

- God is perfect
- A perfect God is an all powerful (omnipotent) God
- An omnipotent God could create a world without any evil
- A perfect God is morally perfect
- A morally perfect God would want to create a world without any evil
- If there is evil in the world, then there is no God
- Experience shows us that there is evil the world
- Therefore, there is no God.[2]

By this account, the problem of evil not only leads to a sense of abandonment by God, but a kind of atheism, a disbelief in God altogether.

Whether there is a sense of abandonment or a newfound atheism, the sufferer, and anyone else asking the same questions, feels distanced from God. The previous belief system about God does not seem to match up with experience and there is a separation from God and from previous beliefs about God. Because God did not intervene and end or prevent the violence, there is alienation from God. Because there are no readily available and satisfactory answers to the questions about God's role in the violence, there is alienation from God. As in my experience, even if there is not explicit anger with God for the perceived absence or betrayal, there can be a deep and empty silence in the face of sexual violence.

To ask the questions: "Why do I suffer?" and "Where is God in my suffering" is to attempt to come to terms with oneself in relation to God and the universe. For those who have experienced sexual violence and for the communities that love them, those questions are often asked in an aching separation from God and within an environment giving different responses from the Bible, our church hymns, the sermons we hear, and the things we say every day.

There are four primary ways to begin to think about questions of suffering and evil:

- Rethink the nature/purpose of evil
- Rethink the omnipotence of God
- Question God's existence
- Question God's goodness or righteousness

These four theological propositions have deep roots and many nuances. In the midst of these options, there are some common responses churches often give to the problem of suffering and evil.

In *Preaching to Sufferers*, Kent Richmond identifies themes that are often heard in church communities. Richmond calls these options "answers that are not." They may or may not be accurate statements about God and the world. They are "answers that are not" because they do nothing to alleviate the pain of the person who hears them.

Suffering is a mystery. This response tends to increase the distance between sufferers and God: When we don't understand suffering, we often say, "Well, it's God's will." When this is said to people who have passed through a time of intense pain, it is not uncommon for them to reply, "Well if that was God's will, then I want nothing to do with God."[3]

Evil is the result of an outside force like Satan. In this scheme, evil is not defeated until a final cosmic battle (Armageddon). True or not, this response does nothing to alleviate the pain of the suffering that is happening right now.

Suffering helps us to appreciate goodness. It is said that we never fully appreciate goodness without evil, or good health without suffering. Some people, however, fail to see any good that can emerge from intense evil and lose faith in all goodness.

Suffering is God's punishment for sin. This ideal falls short in the face of the fact that not all suffering can be traced to sin. A belief in this type of divine punishment can lead to a greater sense of separation from God. The most undeserving, innocent person can feel guilty and may even reject God outright.

Suffering is the way God tests us, teaches us, and strengthens our characters. We often add the reassurance that God does not give people more than they can bear. This kind of response implies that God is responsible, and can only serve to further distance the sufferers from God. This position is also very dangerous because it leads to notions of redemptive suffering. In concepts of redemptive suffering, people believe that suffering brings us closer to God and that there is a greater good behind suffering. Jesus' suffering on the cross is the primary example of redemptive suffering for Christian communities. Theories of redemptive suffering do not always account for the differences between voluntary and involuntary suffering. Whereas Jesus willingly suffered, many people do not choose their suffering. Sexual violence is *always* a situation of involuntary suffering. There is no circumstance under which sexual violence is justifiable; it should *never* happen. The awareness that painful experiences such as sexual violence can be a catalyst for social justice or personal spiritual and emotional growth must *always* come from the victim, not from others.

I don't try to give a perfect answer to these questions. Rather, a ministry addressing sexual violence must be committed to wrestling with the questions. Far too often, we intentionally give some of the earlier "easy answers" in responses to situations of great suffering, without pushing these theologies to their logical conclusions. On the other hand, most churches unintentionally breed multiple responses in the use of various hymns and songs, liturgies and selections of biblical texts. The five previous answers are not just "things we say" to make a tough issue go away. Each of these responses has support from the Bible and lived experience.

In this setting the criterion for responding to questions of evil and suffering must be the "ability to speak to the pain and questions that are brought into the lives of those who suffer."[4]

Some religious scholars believe that there are no adequate answers. They believe that the depth of human suffering is so deep that any justification of it will always trivialize and understate evil.

As churches, we must be willing to sometimes respond to the question with "I don't know." We know what happened, and sometimes how it happened, but we don't know with certainty *why* God let this happen. But a continued belief in the existence of evil is one of the best contributions our tradition has to offer to sufferers. Christianity has never denied evil. We are assured that evil is not an illusion or a product of our imaginations or a misjudgment about others. Evil is real, it is powerful, and it affects the lives of everyone.

This is a good starting point for discussion of suffering and evil.

- There is deep and painful suffering in the lives of individual people and communities.

- We don't know why God allows suffering.
- We must admit that we have some ideas, some proposals, but ultimately we don't know.
- We do know that there is evil, and we do know that the Christian tradition can give us some other fundamental insights by which to live in the meanwhile.

ANOTHER VIEW: GOD IS WITH US AND GOD CARES ABOUT US

The painful work of reconstruction must be done. The difficult work of bringing together God, suffering, and evil is the work that brings the victim back into a relationship with God. This reconstructive work must be done in community. Far too often, the victim of sexual violence is left to do this reconstruction alone. This further isolates the victim. Judith Herman also states that "Not only must [victims] rebuild [their] own 'shattered assumptions' about meaning, order and justice in the world, but [they] must also find a way to resolve [their] differences with those whose beliefs [they] can no longer share."[5] Far too often, the survivor is wrestling and processing these ideas and beliefs alone. Once the survivor finds peace with an answer, it is highly likely that the individual is at a church or in a family that does not share that new belief. Again, the victim-survivor feels alone. The entire community must wrestle with this issue, and reconstruct together.

In the communal reconstruction, the question becomes more difficult. The simple imposition of biblical verses and visions on the human situation today will not suffice for the bloodied souls that sexual violence leaves in its destructive path. These bloodied souls need more than a bandage, more than a transfusion; they need to once again feel the presence and the care of God.

The Dinah Project suggests beginning this reconstruction by *rephrasing the question* for those who experience sexual violence. The better question is:

Where is God in this suffering and what can God do in this situation?[6]

My feelings toward God are numb. I confess I fear God. I feel very much alone and wonder whether there is a loving God out there for me. —*survivor of sexual violence*[7]

Theology must insist on a picture of a close, caring, feeling, present God. The answer to this new question must be a firm unequivocal response:

God is present in suffering with us, and hurting as deeply as we are.[8]

In the face of great incomprehensible evil and suffering, churches can insist on three images of God's character and activity:

- God is with us
- God feels our suffering
- God cares about us

God Is with Us

The concept of God's omnipresence has traditionally been linked to God's omnipotence and God's omniscience. Although omnipresence is defined as an attribute of God such that God "is actually present in all existing places and things," most understandings of omnipresence are not separated from the concept of God as all-powerful, ever-present, and all-knowing. It is possible, however, to separate the concepts. Whereas God's omnipotence and omniscience can be contested in theological circles, belief in God's omnipresence must remain constant.

There is plenty of biblical support for the concept of God's omnipresence. God's presence is transcendent and permeating (Deut. 4:39). God's presence is inescapable (Ps. 139:7–10). Most importantly, God's presence is constant: "When you pass through the waters, I will be with you; and through the rivers, they shall not overwhelm you; when you walk through the fire you shall not be burned, and the flame shall not consume you" (Isa. 43:2).

In the midst of feeling abandoned, it is precisely the presence of God that must be felt. God's presence must remain unquestioned. Churches must portray more than a distant God peering down on earth from above. God's omnipresence is more than a knowledge of all that is occurring. God's presence is an actual nearness. It is intimacy. As the Isaiah passage states, in the most tumultuous of times, we can be assured of God's presence.

The awareness of God's presence can be liberating for those who experience sexual violence. With an omnipresent God, the sufferer can bring the pain of suffering to God. The tradition of the lamenting psalms can be very liberating for sufferers in this manner. In the psalms of lament, we witness the expression of Israel's pain. Rather than turning away from God in the midst of incomprehensible evil, the psalmist takes the pain and abandonment to God. Psalm 22 is one example of the way in which the biblical tradition speaks to the power of bringing the suffering before God:

"My God, my God why have you forsaken me? Why are you so far from helping me, from the words of my groaning? O my God, I cry by day, but you do not answer; and by night, but find no rest" (Ps. 22:1–2).

This psalm describes the sense of utter loneliness, the pain—"I am poured out like water, and all my bones are out of joint; my heart is like wax; it is melted within my breast" (v. 14)—and demands that God respond—"But you, O Lord, do not be far away! O my help, come quickly to my aid!" (v. 19). This type of prayer assumes and insists on God's presence, even when the presence seems distant.

Churches must stress this omnipresence of God even to the point of excess. After all, it is suffering that seems to destroy the awareness of God's presence. Professor of religion Wendy Farley writes: "God is present as the power for redemption in every situation, but suffering can bite so deeply that it is impossible for people to feel its presence; [that is,] nothing separates God from the world, but suffering can be a veil that hides this loving presence."[9] The continual presence of God during a season of pain, suffering, and incomprehension cannot be overstated.

In the act of sexual violence, God is present with the violator *and* the victim. For many of us, this is a difficult concept to accept. Our hearts may naturally empathize and sympathize with the victims of sexual violence. It can be disturbing to think that God is also with the one who was the cause of such pain and anguish. Nevertheless, we must remember that the person who committed the act of sexual violence is still God's creation and God's beloved. The violator is still in need of God's love, grace, and healing power. Our God has not abandoned the victim, but our God has not abandoned the violator either. If ostracized by the church or larger community, violators must know that God has not pushed them from God's embrace of love and compassion.

The church has the challenging task of representing both victims and violators. Both parties often exist within the same congregation, and both parties have the right to a relationship with God. No matter how painful it may be, the church must continue to teach that there is nothing that can separate any of us from the love of God. The church must find a way to offer God's omnipresence to victims, violators, and those who love either one.

Although an emphasis on God's presence is essential, it is not sufficient. The next natural question is about the nature of God's presence. Is God aware and present in the midst of suffering and evil, and just stoic? Does God care about this suffering in which God is so attendant? Does God have any feeling at all in this moment?

God Feels Our Suffering and God Cares for Us

Can God feel? The answer is not obvious. Some parts of our Christian tradition argue that God does not feel. Part of the Christian tradition emphasizes a distant God who is eternal, unmovable, immutable, and unswayed by feeling. If one believes that suffering is part of being imperfect, and God is perfect, then God cannot suffer. One can argue that it is only the human side of Christ that suffers, and not the divine side, because an omnipotent, omniscient God cannot be subject to sorrow and frustration.

An ever-present God must be close and intimate. A distant God who is omnipresent is a God who sees all, and yet cares to do nothing about what is seen. Rather, God intimately enters all aspects of our existence. God does not stand outside of our experiences, knowledgeable of our hurts and pains. When we suffer, God not only knows about our suffering, but God actually feels our suffering. God experiences our pains with us. Our belief that Jesus is the fulfillment of Isaiah's suffering servant gives biblical precedent for this concept of divine suffering. In the image of the suffering servant and the accounts of Jesus' life, death, and resurrection, we see a God who *is* bruised for our iniquities and wounded for our transgressions (Isa. 53:8).

There is some caution in promoting the feeling God. We do not suggest that God is like the gods found in Greek mythology—superhuman gods who are capable of all sorts of emotional disturbances such as jealousy, offense, and sexual urge, and yet who are immortal. When God suffers with and for creation, one can draw out two conclusions that help to reconcile God and the sufferer:

God's own suffering implies that cruelty to others or to ourselves contributes to God's suffering. In this sense, violence against another person or aspect of creation is violence against God. God's divine suffering reminds us of the interconnectedness of our actions. When we sin against one another, we also sin against and hurt God.

God's own suffering helps sufferers to regain their trust in God. In the experience of sexual violence, trust in God is diminished. Those who have experienced sexual violence often lose trust in God to protect them. God can no longer be trusted to rescue them from dangerous situations. This may or not make sense in view of everything else that has been taught about God, but this is the way sexual violence often feels. Trust in God can be reestablished and restrengthened when we realize that God is not unaffected by our suffering.

When I was raped, I lost all sense of trust in God. Less than a year before my rape, I had preached a sermon about being safe inside the will of

God. After the rape, I no longer believed in the scripture I had preached or the words I had written and delivered to a church full of people. In the weeks immediately after the rape, I stumbled through my days looking for any word of encouragement or hope. Almost accidentally, these words came to me and my trust in God was restored. I was sitting at a table in the library trying to focus on the books I had to read and the paper I had to write for a class. I was listening to my personal stereo, flipping radio channels, and I landed on the local gospel station. The radio announcer was reading from Jeremiah 8. I tuned in at the middle of the reading. These are the words I heard: "When I would comfort myself against sorrow, my heart is faint in me. Behold the voice of the cry of the daughter of my people because of them that dwell in a far country: Is not the Lord in Zion? Is not her king in her? Why have they provoked me to anger with their graven images, and with strange vanities? The harvest is past, the summer is ended, and we are not saved. For the hurt of the daughter of my people am I hurt; I am black; astonishment has taken hold on me." I stopped listening then. I was overwhelmed with emotion. There in that library, I began to cry and cry and cry. I heard these words as the words of God to me. For the hurt of the daughter of my people am I hurt. For the first time since I had been raped, I believed that God cared about what happened to me. I had honestly believed that God's failure to protect me was evidence that God no longer cared about me or what had happened to me. Those verses seemed to tell me that God's heart was faint and my hurt had caused God pain as well. I imagined God shedding tears for each of my tears and it was like a rainstorm.

I later realized that the words were from the prophet Jeremiah. I later realized that Jeremiah was mourning over the crisis about the people of Judah. But at that moment, those words restored my trust in God. It was *not* trust that God will protect me from all harm and evil. The new trust is the trust that God cares in every situation and is not neutral, but grieves and hurts with me, with all who suffer. Once I believed that God really cared and really suffered with me, I could start to communicate with God again.

Over time, I have come to my own answers about evil and suffering. Every couple of years, my ideas change as my experiences change. There is one thing that remains constant. Living through the experience of sexual violence and the confusion and pain of the suffering is mitigated by one thing—the capacity of the sufferer to sense the presence of God's love even through the torment.

For those who experience sexual violence and the communities that love them, the questioning is inevitable. Experiences of pain and suffering separate us from God. Even those who have not directly experienced the violence find that their understanding of God, power, evil, goodness, and justice come under scrutiny as they, too, seek to reconcile God and the experience of suffering. As the offenders, violators, and loved ones struggle with this question, they must be assured of the overwhelming presence of God. They must know that God suffers with us and loves us enough to comfort us in our suffering. In the most destructive instances of suffering, the awareness of God's presence is where we find redemption.

12

getting over it: *forgiveness*

No one pressured me to forgive. I was encouraged to "just get over it," much more than I was told to "forgive." My therapist told me that I didn't have to forgive. That contradicted everything I'd ever been taught in church. The church told me to accept apologies and forgive. But the man who raped me never apologized, and my anger put a roadblock in my path to forgiveness.

I was in a better situation than many people. I never had to see my rapist again except the day we dealt with legal issues. I did not have to live in the same community, church, or household with the man who tore my life apart. No one told me to forgive and my hatred towards the man who raped me was tempered by the fact that I had once loved him. Forgiving him was a leisurely decision I made on my own because I just didn't think he deserved all the energy I spent on disliking him.

I don't know the day I forgave him. It didn't happen all at once. Over time, I decided that "who he is" is not determined by what he did to me. I came to think of him as "a man who raped me" more than "a rapist." I knew that there was more to him than this single act—he was another child of God, a son, a brother, a friend. This did not mean that I had to go back to being friends with him. In fact, I prefer to think of him as dead. But this does not mean my process is complete. When I faced him during our legal proceedings I honestly said to him: "Ninety-five percent of the time, I have forgiven you. But, oh, that 5 percent!" That 5 percent creeps in when I hear about how he is doing now or when the anniversary of the rape rolls around. I am bitter, angry, furious, and full of hate. I see this man as the cause of my pain, anguish, tears, and broken relationships. When I look in the mirror, I can almost see steam coming out of my ears. In my eyes, he is evil incarnate. The 5 percent affects me more than it will ever affect him. Forgiveness is for me more than for him.

Ultimately, forgiveness for me meant I was not going to spend my precious time and energy hating this man. For me, forgiveness was the capacity to see this man as more than my rapist. Forgiveness for me meant that this act was not the defining characteristic of who this person is. This is what worked for me. Other people have found my definition of forgiveness too narrow or particular to my own situation. They say that forgiveness is personal and individual. No one can really compare experiences of sexual violence or how people heal or how or if they ever forgive.

In a sense, that is correct. The experience of sexual violence *is* personal and particular to each context and situation. On the other hand, the church must debunk popular incorrect notions about forgiveness: "Forgive and forget." "Try to get along." "Hate the sin and love the sinner." "Forgiveness is for each individual to work through on his or her own." These myths only complicate the already difficult task of thinking of forgiveness in the midst of extreme pain and anger. We cannot leave people alone in this challenging endeavor. As a community, we must rally around those who have experienced sexual violence and make forgiveness a communal event.

WHAT IT FEELS LIKE: HATRED, ANGER, AND DISGUST

This is what he wanted from me—to forgive him? How could I even begin to forgive him? I have loved him! Like a fool, I had loved [the man] I thought he was.
—*family member of survivors and offender of sexual violence*[1]

In the crisis of sexual violence, there is a dramatic separation between the victim and the perpetrator. Although the victim and perpetrator may have ties of family, friendship, or some type of love, the violence has introduced a pain so deep that some level of hatred is inevitable. Whereas some forms of suffering seem to have no obvious source (such as disease, famine, or earthquake), the situation of sexual violence allows the victim to identify and name the source of the trauma. Despite any connection between the violated and violator, sexual violence creates a deep rupture in the victim's understanding about and view toward the violator. The struggle to overcome this rupture is an encounter with the concept of forgiveness.

We must also remember that the victim is not the only party who feels alienated from and angry with the offender. When the community knows the violence, the community, too, must wrestle with forgiveness. Does a community forgive the perpetrator in its midst? They, too, have desires for revenge, forgiveness, compensation, denial, and similar responses. The concept of forgiveness does not remain a one-on-one dialogue. The violence has violated the entire community, and the entire community must deal with the offender.

The concept of forgiveness is first recognized in the process of healing. As long as the sexual violence is denied and internalized, neither the victim nor the victimizer are forced to struggle with the search for peace and communion. Once the violence is acknowledged (either inwardly or publicly), anger, hatred, and disdain for the victimizer is unearthed. These feelings often come to a boil in the process of reconstructing the story of the event(s) of sexual violence. As the story is reconstructed and retold, the victim often feels a desire for vengeance.

Efforts to seek revenge are usually fantasies. Many survivors and their loved ones will initially seek vengeance with the belief that revenge will bring relief. Rather than bringing relief, attempts to seek revenge increase torment and do not alleviate post-traumatic symptoms. Ultimately, people will realize that it is impossible to "get even," and they may transform that energy into righteous indignation. Vengeance is a misguided attempt at empowerment.

WHAT WE HAVE BEEN TAUGHT: JUST GET OVER IT

Those who feel that they have been violated in the experience of sexual violence feel both a desire and obligation to forgive. Although forgiveness is part of the healing process, forgiving will not eradicate the pain of the trauma. That is an unhealthy desire to forgive. In addition to this unhealthy desire to forgive, there is the Christian obligation to forgive.

Christian teaching says that we have an ethical duty to forgive and it is connected to God's willingness to forgive us. This understanding can be traced to the petition in the Lord's prayer, "Forgive us our trespasses as we forgive those who trespass against us." The message is that God will not forgive us if we do not forgive the people who hurt us. In the context of sexual violence, the victim can easily conclude that one must forgive, and forgive immediately, or else his or her faith becomes void and empty.

Those who feel violated are not the only ones desiring the ability to forgive. The perpetrator may also desire forgiveness from the victim and community. Many times, forgiveness is viewed as an immediate way to be relieved of guilt for wrongful actions.[2] Some offenders will request forgiveness: "An offender may approach a pastor seeking forgiveness or may ask the victim to forgive. Usually these requests are accompanied by genuine remorse and promises of changed behavior."[3] If the offender acknowledges guilt and expresses remorse, the victim's resistance to forgive is a roadblock to the perpetrator's healing as well. As persons who are familiar with not only the command to forgive, but the need to be forgiven, a denial of forgiveness can have a significant spiritual impact on the offender.

Many of our thoughts about forgiveness do not come directly from the Bible. The four most popular notions about forgiveness are not found within the biblical scriptures:

- Forgive and forget
- Hate the sin and love the sinner
- Kiss and make up
- Deal with it on your own

These ideas about forgiveness contradict almost every context of contention between human beings. They are particularly unhelpful in the case of sexual violence.

Forgive and Forget

The violence is impossible to forget. Even if one tried, the violence is remembered in the subconscious, in the bodily memory, in the remembrance of the smells and sounds surrounding the event. Psychologists agree that forgetfulness is not recommended. Reconstructing and remembering the violence assures the victim, victimizer, and surrounding community of what really happened, and it encourages them to take steps to ensure that it does not happen again. In constructive remembering, individuals and communities can take steps to ensure greater safety and to seek justice for all people who have been deeply hurt by others.

Hate the Sin and Love the Sinner

The charge to hate the sin and love the sinner is asking a nearly impossible task of people whose lives have been shattered by the actions of one person. The courage to love one's own self after violation is challenging; the call to love the violator is simply cruel. Love is an act of the heart. There is no reason to expect victims of sexual violence to make any room in their hearts for the person who has violated them. Feelings of anger and hatred are natural responses to the trauma that accompanies sexual violence. To deny these feelings to the many people who are angry and hurt by incidents of sexual violence is to deny them a critical step in their process of healing. It is to deny them the right to their humanity.

Kiss and Make Up

We often conflate the concepts of forgiveness and reconciliation. There is a Christian duty to forgive, but there is no duty to reconcile. Reconciliation is the restoration of a relationship after a violation has occurred. Reconciliation may not be safe or wise for those who have experienced sexual violence. Maintaining a relationship with the abusive person may only result in repeated occasions of violence. Communicating and fellowship with the violator does not mean that there are not feelings of anger, resentment, and hatred, and a refusal to forgive. The decision about whether or not to reconcile should be separated from the concept of forgiveness. Asking people who have experienced sexual violence to begin or restore a relationship of communication or fellowship with the violator may be asking people to return to the deepest places of their pain and trauma.

Deal with It on Your Own

Most commonly, we assume that forgiveness is an act that an individual miraculously conducts alone and internally. We think that forgiveness is something that people need to settle in the heart on their own. We think about forgiveness as something that is worked out between God and an individual person, or between one person and another. No one else should meddle or interfere aside from issuing the reminder that people have to forgive because God said so.

ANOTHER VIEW: FORGIVENESS IS A COMMUNAL EVENT

Some scholars and therapists do not believe victims must forgive. Judith Lewis Herman states that survivors should not have to forgive. She believes that forgiveness is only necessary when the violator apologizes and makes steps to heal and repent. This type of contrition is rare. Thus Herman suggests that survivors do not even attempt acts of forgiveness because they are impediments to healing and are nearly impossible to actualize. She states that a process of grieving and mourning the losses are more appropriate approaches to dealing with the violence that has occurred.

Herman is correct in her assessment that the trauma cannot be exorcised through hatred or love. Herman and others who believe similarly honor the very real feeling of resistance to forgiving. They honor the depth of the pain that can lead to a conclusion of irreconcilable differences. But they forget that many of us have been raised with the Christian edict to forgive. Forgiving is part of what makes us "good Christians." We can't just eradicate the concept of forgiveness from a Christian tradition that stresses its importance and necessity.

Marie Fortune is the only scholar in the study of sexual violence that consistently examines the struggle to forgive. First, she redefines forgiveness. "Forgiveness is letting go of the immediacy of the trauma, the memory of which continues to terrorize the victim and limit possibilities; . . . [it is] putting the memory into perspective so that it no longer dominates one's life."[4] Second, Fortune establishes criteria for forgiveness. Fortune also asserts that there are prerequisites to forgiveness. Fortune gives biblical support. In Luke 17:3–4, Jesus is recorded as making this oft-quoted statement on forgiveness: "Be on your guard! If another disciple sins, you must rebuke the offender, and if there is repentance, you must forgive. And if the same person sins against you seven times a day, and turns back to you seven times and says 'I repent,' you must forgive."

Based on this passage, Fortune finds three preconditions for forgiveness that she calls "justice":

- Confession—acknowledgment that harm has been done to one person by another
- Repentance—a fundamental change that necessarily requires more than good intentions, but time, hard work, and therapy
- Restitution—the responsibility of the abuser to provide materially for the restoration of those who have been harmed[5]

Fortune does acknowledge the fact that the violator may never come to stages of confession, repentance, and restitution. These biblically expanded criteria for forgiveness still tie the victim's healing to the actions of the violator. If a violator never seeks forgiveness, does this mean that forgiveness is no longer necessary?

Forgive/Embrace: What the Community Must Do

No. Forgiveness has always been addressed in the context of absolving sin. In its broadest definition, sin is anything that separates us from fellowship with God and each other. Sexual violence brings sin into the world because of the way in which it alienates and separates individuals from their own bodies, from God, and from each other. The worst aspect of sexual violence is the silence, secrecy, and shame—the sense that no one else can understand the feelings of those who have experienced sexual violence. Sexual violence is sinful because it pulls people out of fellowship with God and other people.

If forgiveness breaks the grasp of sin, then forgiveness should draw individuals back into fellowship with God and others. The church community contains the first step for forgiveness. Forgiveness is the process of the community embracing those people who have experienced sexual violence. This is no easy task, as the community must forgive/embrace the violated, the violator and all those who love them. The call to forgive/embrace means that church communities should not mock or ostracize or ignore those who have experienced sexual violence. It means getting over the awkwardness, the feelings of ill will and discomfort and anger to remind individuals that they are still part of the family of God.

In the particular case of sexual violence, forgiveness on the part of the community means that the community can strive to make justice with those who have been violated. Fortune suggests a community do the following things:

- Acknowledge the harm done to the victim
- Break the silence about sexual violence
- Hear and believe the experience of victims, thereby standing in solidarity with victims
- Protect the vulnerable[6]

Standing in solidarity with victims is an act of forgiveness. Taking a stand against sexual violence is an act of forgiveness. In these activities, the community refuses to leave the victims in isolation and despair. Forgiveness refuses to leave the violators outside the community.

Although the community has an important role to play in the process of forgiveness, there is an individual role as well. Every person must come to a place of forgiveness. When forgiveness is a communal event, forgiving is the ability to recognize another person as a member of a community. Asking people to forgive in the context of sexual violence is not asking people to love one another, or have lunch and small talk with another person. Forgiveness is asking people to release the myopia of their pain and personal experiences. The intense pain and betrayal of sexual violence easily renders another person as "the rapist," or "the offender." The person becomes defined by the violation she or he has committed. When we think of an individual only in the circumstances of the abuse, we deny people the opportunity to heal, transform, or change. We deny God the opportunity to transform and change them. We deny them their rights to love and fellowship and community. Individual forgiveness is finding the ability to see the violator as part of a community. The violator may well be a rapist, but the violator is also someone's child, someone's sibling, perhaps even someone's parent. The violator is still a created child of God.

Expanding one's vision beyond the context of sexual violence is challenging. It is not the work of the heart or the will alone. It cannot be done alone. As we live and heal and wrestle and mourn together in and through community, we are positioned to receive the grace and mercy of God that enables us to see a broader picture. We understand that just as we are part of a community, and that community draws us deeper into relationship with God and each other, so the people we want to detest and loathe are also part of that community.

This communal event of forgiveness is not a single act. It is a process. Forgiveness takes time. Immediately after an assault, or even during the remembrance and mourning of the assault, the anger, pain, and hatred are raw and intense. The longing or obligation to forgive is overwhelmed by the very real sense of not *feeling* forgiving.[7] Forgiveness is *the last step* in the process of healing. Forgiveness takes time and it may have to be revisited time and time again. An entire community may feel as I often do— 95 percent of the time forgiveness has been achieved, but there is still 5 percent of resentment, anger, and a desire to banish violators to solitude.

Remember that forgiveness is a challenging issue in any context. It is, arguably, the most difficult thing that God asks of us. Like the questions of evil and suffering, there are few simple answers. Ministries that address sexual violence must be willing to collectively struggle with, debate, contest, feel confused about, and work on this topic of forgiveness. Such struggling is not an indication of a lack of faith. Rather it is an indication that this faith community takes seriously the many dimensions of the lived Christian faith.

Invited speakers and workshops leaders can greatly contribute to the church's understanding of forgiveness. Fresh voices and new perspectives always assist in the process of discernment and understanding. Always give care to listen to the experiences of those who have experienced sexual violence and accept them where they are in their process of healing, finding peace, and forgiving. The Dinah Project is concerned with honoring the pain of those who experience sexual violence, and honoring the process of recovery. Recovery is slow, but attainable. Sexual violence causes all of us to rethink what we know about sexuality, safety, God, and forgiveness. The entire community will heal when we covenant to journey there together.

13

time, prayer, and grace

Planning and organization is crucial to organizing a ministry to respond to the controversial issue of sexual violence, but eventually all ministries rely on the passage of time, lots of prayer, and the grace of God to pull everything together. I want to share a story.

Sometime, not that long ago, I had a bad day. But I don't really have bad days; I have bad nights. I had awakened around 1:00 in the morning after a nightmare and I was terrified. Not scared, but terrified and paralyzed. The walls and the doors and the windows seemed paper-thin and I felt vulnerable to the world around me. And it was a terror that I didn't know how to voice. I didn't know whom to call. How do you explain what you can't explain, and that for some reason on that day at that particular time, I was terrified. So I stayed awake as long as I could and I wasn't going back to sleep. Eventually my body overcame my fears and I fell asleep. I woke up just a couple hours later because I had to get up and go to work. The world didn't stop just because I had.

On my way out the door, I walked by a plant that sits outside my front door. Now I don't have the greenest thumb but I like to keep plants around me. Some people have children, some people have pets, and I have my plants. And so I name my plants. I named my first plant "Life" because no matter what I did to it, or forgot to do for it, it would not die. Over time, I got "Energy" and "Passion" and "Courage" and "Mercy." I have no systematic way of naming my plants. I just look at them and see what I feel and that's what I call them. But the plants and their conditions always seem to represent their names in my life.

I eventually acquired a small aloe vera plant that I named "Healing." It seemed reasonable since the aloe from the plant is so well known for its ability to heal cuts and burns. Healing had been doing particularly well, growing quite large, and so I thought that Healing could use a new home. I transplanted Healing into a larger pot and placed it in a sunny, but not too sunny place, and Healing began to grow. After a little while, Healing wasn't doing too well—leaves were getting a little brown, and new leaves stopped showing up. I got very concerned and I talked to Healing more and began to encourage Healing: "You can do it! Don't give up! Grow!" And Healing still wasn't doing too well. I tried to water Healing more and that didn't work. So I stopped watering Healing as much and that didn't work.

I began to call in the experts. I called in my friends who were farmers, gardeners, and experts in biology and agriculture. "Come look at my plant," I said. "Something is wrong." I went to the store and bought the plant food and everything, but still Healing was not doing so well. I was concerned because I want all my plants to live and to thrive, and Healing just wasn't. As Healing descended into disease, I looked up one day and there was a mushroom and some bugs around Healing. Now I love my plants, but I really don't like bugs inside my house. I just couldn't take that. So I decided that Healing would have to go outside and fend for itself.

I knew that it was not past the last frost of winter in Tennessee and that even after the advent of spring, it was still going to get cold outside. But I decided that the plant could not stay in my house because I was not going to have mushrooms and insects germinating in my house. So I put Healing on the front porch and refused to do anything more for Healing. I thought, "I have given this plant all this energy, I have called the experts, but I can do no more for this plant. If it dies, it dies. And I'll buy another one. I mean, it's just an aloe vera plant." And the first frost had come and gone, and my plant-expert friends gawked at what I had done—"Don't you know it is still cold?!" I shrugged my shoulders at them saying, "Yes, but it had to be done." Tornado warnings were posted, major storms came through. Outside, Healing had been flooded; Healing's leaves had dropped.

And this particular morning, after my series of nightmares and fears and night terrors, I noticed that there were still four green shoots on Healing. Three were clustered together and one was bending upwards, and I looked down and I realized that Healing was not dead. Floods had come, winds has come, storms had come, very cold weather had come, but Healing was not dead. The experts had come and gone, I had neglected Healing, I had tried to help Healing, but Healing was not dead. And in that moment, I remembered that I should never underestimate the power of God's creation to strive for life.

When I was raped, I thought I was dead. I was dead to myself and I felt dead to the world. I have heard sentiments like my own echoed by people with whom I have spoken across the country. "It's like being the walking dead." But the good news is that, like my plant, healing is not dead. There are still some green shoots in healing. Frosts will come and go. The winds will blow, telephone wires will be knocked down, floods will come into our lives, but healing is not dead.

If The Dinah Project says nothing else, the message is that healing is not dead.

Even when we give up on our healing, put ourselves out of our own houses and places of comfort and refuge, healing will not die. We can never underestimate the power that God put in all of us to strive for life.

There is life after sexual violence.

There is life after breaking the silence.

In the beginning, The Dinah Project was little more than a notion in my head. As the years went on, Dinah became more than an idea, and more than a project. Dinah became real. Statistics say that it is one in four women and one in six boys and one in twelve men. But those are numbers. When we look at our programs and if you go through our files, you will see names and cases. They are names and numbers. What I see when I look at The Dinah Project is the stories. Over time, people have welcomed me into their lives, into their stories, and into their processes. This is Dinah.

Doing something like The Dinah Project ultimately brings with it feelings of insecurity and risk. It might feel like putting a baby in a reed basket and sending it up the Nile River. But Dinah does not belong to any one person. Dinah is a child of the entire church. I have often boasted that The Dinah Project has the best volunteers. I cannot count the number of people from the church and the community who have asked, "What can I do?" and welcomed me into their hearts and have said, "This is something I want to be a part of."

Dinah has grown from an infant into a toddler walking and talking and getting into things all on her own. Dinah has grown into an independently willed school-age child walking off into the horizon turning around and saying, "Are you coming or not?" Dinah has grown to become someone that Metropolitan Interdenominational Church claims as its child. Dinah is someone that the city of Nashville, Tennessee, has welcomed as one of its own. Dinah grew from a small idea and a worship service into community education, into workshops and presentations across the country and radio programs and group counseling. These things are made possible because of the generosity, understanding, willingness, commitment, and sometimes just the blind intrigue about what Dinah might have said and what Dinah might have wanted.

And if the church ends silence in the church about sexuality in general and sexual violence in particular, then that is Dinah. If the church can create a space where you can trust someone, where you can walk in and lose your mind and still walk out with your dignity intact, then that is Dinah. If the church can help us to see that sexual violence is not a women's issue or a man's issue or an adult issue, but it is everybody's issue, then that is Dinah. And if the church can make the difference between blocking God out of your pain and inviting God into your life, then you have found Dinah. If you have made the difference between giving up on this place we call church and staying dedicated that somewhere, somebody who stands behind this pulpit cares, then you have sat with Dinah. If the church can shift the question from "God, where were you?" to "God, I know this hurts you too," then that is Dinah. If the church begins to run towards its challenges and embrace and argue and cry and laugh over its most difficult doctrines and hard-to-love members, then that is Dinah.

This does not happen overnight. It takes time, patience, prayer, and a deep-seated belief that healing is not dead. I believe in Dinah because I have seen it happen and I know that, in a little church on a hill, it has occurred not once or twice, but time and time again. Following this bold child into the horizon will be a joy and a challenge. It will entail frustration, sadness, and grief. But it will be a blessing. The only way to truly address sexual violence in the church is through passion, time, prayer, and ultimately by the gracious, creative, and transformative power of the God we serve.

I would like to know about the ways you have embraced Dinah in your own church. I am also available for presentations, lectures, sermons, and other services. Please contact me at www.MonicaAColeman.com.

APPENDIX A

Doing Your Homework—
Where to Get Information

INTERNET RESOURCES
General Information

- The Rape, Abuse & Incest National Network (RAINN)—one stop shop site for updated information on sexual violence
  http://www.rainn.org
- A page off that site that will guide you to local crisis centers
  http://analog.atlantic-records.com/crisiscenters/default.asp
- Minnesota Center Against Violence and Abuse—amazing information and resources
  http://www.mincava.umn.edu
- Violence Against Women Office
  http://www.vaw.umn.edu
- Violence Against Women National Electronic Network
  http://www.vawnet.org
- National Sexual Violence Resource Center
  http://www.nsvrc.org
- For the serious researcher, a site in collaboration with the Center for Disease Control (CDC)
  http://www.vawprevention.org

For Teenagers and College Students

- Sexual Assault Education for students
  http://www.healthy-dating.com

Family Violence and Incest

- Stop Family Violence
  http://stopfamilyviolence.org
- Incest Survivors
  http://www.voices-action.org
- Preventing Child Sexual Abuse
  http://www.stopitnow.org

Programs Targeting Men

- Men Stopping Violence—great resources, training, and program
  http://www.menstoppingviolence.org
- Domestic Violence Intervention Center (formerly PEACE
  (Project to End Abuse through Counseling and Education)—
  group counseling with male perpetrators
  http://www.state.tn.us/youth/online_services/SOSweb/Davidson/
  dvic_dom_dc.htm
- Men Can Stop Rape
  http://www.mencanstoprape.org
- MOVE—Men Overcoming Violence
  http://www.menresourcecenter.org/move.html
- Association for the Treatment of Sexual Abusers
  http://www.atsa.com

More on Post Traumatic Stress Disorder (PTSD)

- Gift From Within
  http://www.giftfromwithin.org
- PTSD Alliance
  http://www.ptsdalliance.org

Organizations that Look at Religion/Christianity and Sexual Violence

- Religious Coalition for Reproductive Choice—Not just about
  abortion issues. The Black Church Initiative may be of interest to
  some congregations.
  http://www.rcrc.org
- Interfaith Sexual Trauma Institute—Focuses, but not exclusively,
  on clergy sexual misconduct. Primarily from the perspective of
  scholars and clergy
  http://www.csbsju.edu/isti

- Faith/Trust Institute (formerly Center for the Prevention of Sexual and Domestic Violence)—One of the best resources for books and training for churches, clergy, and laity from a Jewish and Christian perspective
  http://www.cpsdv.org
- Tamar's Voice—Focuses exclusively on the experience of clergy sexual misconduct—primarily from the perspective of survivors. Has a good newsletter.
  http://www.tamarsvoice.org
- The Dinah Project—An organized church response to sexual violence in the community
  http://www.metropolitanfrc.com/dinah_project.asp
- The Black Church Domestic Violence—Focuses on the black church's role in improving the quality of life for victims of sexual and domestic violence
  http://www.bcdvi.org

PRINT RESOURCES

My Favorite Books

Herman, Judith Lewis. *Trauma and Recovery: The Aftermath of Violence—From Domestic Abuse to Political Terror*. New York: BasicBooks, 1992. My favorite for good basic information about the experience of trauma from a social-psychological perspective.

Fortune, Marie M. *Sexual Violence: The Unmentionable Sin, An Ethical and Pastoral Perspective*. New York: Pilgrim Press, 1983. Groundbreaking work that is still important, and written very clearly.

Poling, James. *The Abuse of Power: A Theological Problem*. Nashville: Abingdon, 1991. Examines the way in which the abuse of power in wider culture and in the church contribute to the prevalence of sexual violence in our society.

Adams, Carol J., and Marie M. Fortune, eds. *Violence Against Women and Children: A Christian Theological Sourcebook*. New York: Continuum, 1995. Good feminist analysis of the interplay of theology and violence.

Books for Pastors

Cooper-White, Pamela. *The Cry of Tamar: Violence Against Women and the Church's Response*. Minneapolis: Fortress Press, 2003.

Kroeger, Catherine Clark, and James R. Beck. *Women, Abuse and the Bible: How Scripture Can Be Used to Hurt or to Heal.* Grand Rapids: Baker Book House, 1996.

Leslie, Kristen J. *When Violence is No Stranger: Pastoral Counseling with Survivors of Acquaintance Rape.* Minneapolis: Fortress Press, 2002.

Livingston, David J. *Healing Violent Men: A Model for Christian Communities.* Minneapolis: Fortress Press, 2003.

McClintock, Karen A. *Sexual Shame: An Urgent Call to Healing.* Minneapolis: Fortress Press, 2003.

Means, J. Jeffrey, and Mary Ann Nelson. *Trauma and Evil: Healing the Wounded Soul.* Minneapolis: Fortress Press, 2003.

Miles, Al. *Domestic Violence: What Every Pastor Needs to Know.* Minneapolis: Fortress Press, 2000.

Miles, Al. *Violence in Families: What Every Christian Should Know.* Minneapolis: Fortress Press, 2002.

Books for Churches

McClure, John S., and Nancy J. Ramsay, eds. *Telling the Truth: Preaching and Sexual and Domestic Violence.* Cleveland: United Church Press, 1998. One of the first books that help pastors to bring their responses to sexual violence out of the pastoral counseling session and into the broader church community. There are three publications that work with churches in a workbook fashion.

Fortune, Marie M., and Rebecca Voekel-Haugen. *Sexual Abuse Prevention: A Course of Study for Teenagers.* Cleveland: United Church Press, 1996. A good tool for working in an ongoing setting such as a Bible study or church school. It is specifically designed for those who work with the teenage population.

Fortune, Marie M. *Violence in the Family: A Workshop Curriculum for Clergy and Other Helpers.* Cleveland: Pilgrim Press, 1991. A thorough curriculum designed for clergy and other church leaders. Utilizing this book requires a deep commitment to education and long-term changes on the part of clergy and church members.

Miller, Melissa A. *Family Violence: The Compassionate Church Response.* Scottdale, Pa.: Herald Press, 1994. Brings the issue of sexual violence to a broad cross-section of a church's membership. The book is intended for leaders of small church groups—adult church school classes, elders, deacon groups, fellowship groups, and ministerial fellowships.

Pellauer, Mary D., Barbara Chester, and Jane A. Boyajin. *Sexual Assault and Abuse: A Handbook for Clergy and Religious Professionals.* New York: Harper & Row, 1987 (out of print). Provides essays on different aspects of the religious implications of sexual violence, with accompanying litanies that can be used in church settings.

Other Books of Note

Adams, Carol J. *Woman Battering.* Minneapolis: Fortress Press, 1997.

Bass, Ellen. *I Never Told Anyone: A Collection of Writings by Women Survivors of Sexual Child Abuse.* New York: HarperCollins, 1993.

Bass, Ellen, and Laura Davis. *The Courage to Heal: A Guide for Women Survivors of Child Sexual Abuse.* New York: Harper and Row, 1988.

Blumenthal, David R. *Facing the Abusing God: A Theology of Protest.* Louisville: Westminster John Knox Press, 1993.

Brown, Joanne Carlson, and Carole R. Bohn, eds. *Christianity, Patriarchy, and Abuse.* Cleveland: Pilgrim Press, 1989.

Buchwald, Emilie, Pamela R. Fletcher, and Martha Roth, eds. *Transforming a Rape Culture.* Minneapolis: Milkweed Editions, 1993.

Burgess, Ann Wolbert, and Lynda Lytle Holstrom. *Rape: Victims of Crisis.* Bowie, Md.: Robert J. Brady Company, 1974.

Burns, Maryviolet, ed. *The Speaking Profits Us: Violence in the Lives of Women of Color.* Seattle: The Center for the Prevention of Sexual and Domestic Violence, 1986.

Butler, Sandra. *Conspiracy of Silence.* San Francisco: New Glide Publications, 1978.

Byerly, Carolyn. *The Mother's Book.* Dubuque, Ia.: Kendall/Hunt Publishing, 1985.

Feldmeth, Joanne Ross, and Midge W. Finley. *We Weep for Ourselves and Our Children: A Christian Guide for Survivors of Childhood Sexual Abuse.* San Francisco: HarperSanFrancisco, 1990.

Finkelhor, David. *Child Sexual Abuse: New Theory and Research.* New York: Free Press (Macmillan), 1984.

Fortune, Marie M. *Keeping the Faith: Questions and Answers for the Abused Woman.* San Francisco: HarperSanFrancisco, 1987.

Fortune, Marie M. "Violence against Women: The Way Things Are Is Not the Way They Have to Be" in *Sexuality and the Sacred: Sources for Theological Reflection.* Ed. James B. Nelson and Sandra P. Longfellow. Louisville: Westminster John Knox Press, 1994.

Fortune, Marie M. *Is Nothing Sacred? When Sex Invades the Pastoral Relationship.* San Francisco: HarperSanFrancisco, 1989.

Fortune, Marie M., and James Poling. *Sexual Abuse by Clergy: A Crisis for the Church.* Decatur, Ill.: Journal of Pastoral Care Publications, 1993.

Heggen, Carolyn H. *Sexual Abuse in Christian Homes and Churches.* Scottdale, Pa.: Herald Press, 1993.

Hermann, Judith. *Father-Daughter Incest.* Cambridge: Harvard University Press, 1982.

Huff, Margaret Edith Craddock. *Woman in the Image of God: Towards a Prototype for Feminist Pastoral Counseling.* Ann Arbor, Mich.: UMI, 1990.

Keene, Jane. *A Winter's Song: A Liturgy for Women Seeking Healing from Sexual Abuse in Childhood.* New York: Pilgrim Press, 1991.

Lebacqz, Karen, and Ronald G. Barton. *Sex in the Parish.* Louisville: Westminster John Knox Press, 1991.

Lebacqz, Karen, and David Guinn. *Sexuality: A Reader.* Cleveland: Pilgrim Press, 2000.

Lew, Mike. *Victims No Longer.* New York: Harper & Row, 1988.

MacDonald, John M. *Rape: Controversial Issues—Criminal Profiles, Date Rape, False Reports and False Memories.* Springfield, Ill.: Charles C. Thomas, 1995.

Madigan, Lee, and Nancy C. Gamble. *The Second Rape: Society's Continued Betrayal of the Victim.* New York: Lexington Books, 1989.

Maltz, Wendy, and Beverly Holman. *Incest and Sexuality: A Guide to Understanding and Healing.* Lexington, Ky.: Lexington Books, 1987.

Milgrom, Jeanette Hofstee. *Boundaries in Professional Relationships: A Training Manual.* Minneapolis: Walk-In Counseling Center, 1992.

Parrot, Andrea, and Laurie Bechhoker, eds. *Acquaintance Rape: The Hidden Crime.* New York: John Wiley & Sons, 1991.

Pellauer, Mary D., and Susan Brooks Thistlethwaite. "Conversation on Grace and Healing: Perspectives from the Movement to End Violence Against Women" in *Lift Every Voice: Constructing Christian Theologies from the Underside.* Ed. Susan Brooks Thistlethwaite and Mary Potter Engel. New York: Harper & Row, 1990.

Ramsay, Nancy J. "Sexual Abuse and Shame: The Travail of Recovery" in *Women in Travail and Transition: A New Pastoral Care.* Ed. Maxine Glaz and Jeanne Stevenson Moessner. Minneapolis: Fortress Press, 1991.

Ramshaw, Elaine. *Ritual and Pastoral Care.* Minneapolis: Fortress Press, 1987.

Robinson, Lori S. *I Will Survive: The African-American Guide to Healing from Sexual Assault and Abuse.* Seattle: Seal Press, 2003.

Rose, Tricia. *Longing to Tell: Black Women Talk About Sexuality and Intimacy.* New York: Farrar, Straus & Giroux, 2003.

Rush, Florence. *The Best Kept Secret: Sexual Abuse of Children.* Summit, Pa.: TAB Books (McGraw-Hill), 1981.

Russell, Diana E. H. *The Politics of Rape: The Victim's Perspective.* New York: Stein and Day, 1979.

Russell, Diana E. H. *Rape in Marriage.* New York: Macmillan, 1983.

Rutter, Peter. *Sex in the Forbidden Zone.* Los Angeles: Jeremy P. Torcher, 1989.

Sewell, Marilyn. *Cries of the Spirit: A Celebration of Women's Spirituality.* Boston: Beacon Press, 1991.

Trible, Phyllis. *Texts of Terror.* Philadelphia: Fortress Press, 1984.

West, Traci C. *Wounds of the Spirit: Black Women, Violence and Resistance Ethics.* New York: New York University Press, 1999.

Wilson, Melba. *Crossing the Boundary: Black Women Survive Incest.* Seattle: Seal Press, 1993.

PUBLICITY OUTREACH FOCUS

Organizations

Program focusing on recovery from drugs for women
Ministers' fellowship organization
Domestic violence program
Program focusing on recovery from drugs
Local rape crisis center
YWCA
Local college police
Local divinity school
Another local seminary

Press

Listing of local papers with contact names of religion editors and fax numbers

Radio

Radio stations with phone numbers and fax numbers

Churches who may be interested in collaboration

List of local church with pastor's name

Appendix B

Getting Organized —
Job Descriptions and Other Resources

INVITATION TO JOIN ADVISORY BOARD

Dear Prospective Dinah Project Advisory Board Member:

You are invited to an important meeting of The Dinah Project Advisory Board. Because of your interest and gifts, the pastor, [insert name], and myself have identified you as one who may be able to give greatly to the work of The Dinah Project. We will be meeting on [date] at [time] at the church, [church address] (Breakfast provided!).

At this meeting we will be brought up to date on the status and activities of The Dinah Project in the last year, and share our vision and tasks for the immediate and longer range future of The Dinah Project. In particular, we will be working on vision and mission statements, but we will also be doing some more concrete event planning as well.

Please think about directions and ideas you have for The Dinah Project, and any gifts or resources you may bring to this special ministry.
I believe that together we make ministry everybody's business just as The Dinah Project belongs to this entire church and community!

If you have any questions, feel free to call me. *Please reply*; you can reach me at home at [insert number] or via e-mail at [e-mail address]. I look forward to seeing you there!

[name of project coordinator]
project coordinator

AGENDA FOR ADVISORY BOARD MEETING

The Dinah Project
[church name]
[date]

Opening prayer and centering moment
[advisory board member]

Introductory remarks
[pastor]
The Dinah Project—vision and program
[project coordinator]

Role of the Advisory Committee (reference to the mailing)
[project coordinator]

The Dinah Project as part of the overall ministries of the church
[church minister]

Discussion
[everyone]

Next scheduled Dinah Project event—[date]
Summary and closure

VISION STATEMENT

We envision a world where

- the church is the first, not the last place where persons come whose lives have been diminished by sexual violence;
- sexual violence is understood as everybody's violation;
- legal, medical, and social service agencies work together with the church to provide holistic healing to those affected by sexual violence;
- all come to know a God who specializes in transforming lives and who intimately cares.

MISSION STATEMENT

Because we believe that the church should be a safe place where God's redemptive message brings comfort and healing to those who mourn, our mission is to:

Take collective responsibility for the crime, prevention, and healing of sexual violence; combat the silence associated with incest, child sexual abuse, sexual assault, and rape; provide safe places for healing with integrated models of care for the soul, spirit, mind, and body.

Restore a sense of wholeness and health for victims, violators, and those who love them, addressing the spiritual and theological crises borne out of the experience of sexual violence.

Promote healthy attitudes about sex and relationships, celebrating the gift of sexuality within the context of healthy emotional and spiritual development.

JOB DESCRIPTIONS FOR A GRANT PROPOSAL

Project Coordinator (full-time position)

The project coordinator is responsible for the daily operation and implementation of the ministry, including supervision of staff and volunteers. This person serves as the principal community educator, representing the ministry and the church. This person will provide assistance to the therapist in defining and addressing spiritual and theological issues for clients. Essential to this position are: Master of Divinity degree, ordained clergy credentials, experience and knowledge of spiritual and theological effects of sexual violence, program management and supervisory skills and experience, excellent communication skills, and community organizing or coalition building experience.

Therapist (full-time position)

The therapist is responsible for the delivery of therapeutic services to clients, including group and individual counseling. This person conducts intakes and assessments of clients and develops a plan of care with clients. The therapist assists the project coordinator in providing community education. Essential skills to this position are: Master of Social Work or comparable certification, two years experience with victims and/or perpetrators of sexual violence, community education skills, training and experience in group and individual therapy, sensitivity to spiritual and theological effects of sexual violence, excellent communication skills, case management, and database experience.

Administrative Assistant (half-time position)

The administrative assistant is responsible for performing clerical and administrative functions for the ministry, including maintaining client files, observing confidentiality policies and procedures, and scheduling community education. Essential skills for this program are: high school diploma or GED, one-year secretarial/clerical experience including user knowledge of general office machines, typing fifty words per minute, and proficient computer skills, including database experience. Medical records management preferred.

Fiscal Manager (quarter-time position)

The fiscal manager will assist the project coordinator in administering the budget and financial matters as relates to the ministry and church. This person insures compliance with required financial and audit reporting. Essential skills include: Bachelor's degree, general accounting and book-keeping experience, including grants management skills and experience, and computer proficiency in financial management software.

APPENDIX C

Saying "Rape" in the Sanctuary— Worship Service Aids

SAMPLE PRESS RELEASES

Community Recognition Service Press Release

For Immediate Release
[church name]
The Dinah Project:

An organized church response to the crisis of sexual violence in our communities.

A worship service for the community recognition of sexual violence in our midst.

[date]
6:00–7:30 P.M.
[church name]
[address]
[phone number]

[Name of keynote speaker/preacher], [short biographical sketch of the speaker/preacher], will be the guest speaker for the evening.

This service is the first of three worship services focusing on the themes of:

- Community Recognition
- Forgiveness
- Healing

The Dinah Project provides educational workshops for clergy and laity to promote awareness and appropriate response to the crisis of sexual violence in the community. The Dinah Project also coordinates worship services and counseling designed to address the spiritual and theological issues for the victims, perpetrators, and the communities that love them. By refusing to perpetuate the silence associated with incest, child sexual abuse, sexual assault, and rape, The Dinah Project hopes to address the spiritual and theological crises of sexual violence that few professionals currently provide.

[Here you want a quote from someone at the church. An example follows.]

Rev. Monica A. Coleman, of [church name], says, "We hope and pray that The Dinah Project will help us to take collective responsibility for the crime, prevention, and healing of sexual violence in our midst. We believe that the church and the community of faith should be a safe place to mourn and heal from this tragedy in the world."

Service of Forgiveness Press Release

For Immediate Release
Contact: [project coordinator]
Phone: [phone number]

A Church Response to Sexual Violence

[Name of church] is proud to present The Dinah Project, a three-part organized, spiritual response to the manifestations of sexual violence in our communities. On [date], there will be a workshop and worship service that address the complexity of forgiveness in the context of sexual violence. The workshop will be held at 3:30–4:30 P.M. to be followed by a worship service at 5:00–7:00 P.M. Both activities will be held at the [church name and address], where [pastor's name] is the pastor.

[Name of speaker], [degree], [some biographical information] will be the guest speaker for the workshop and worship service. [Name of speaker] is [more biographical information].

This workshop and service commemorate the second of three worship moments that seek to bring together the church and issues of sexual violence.

[Here you want a quote from someone at the church. An example follows.] Rev. Monica A. Coleman, a pastoral assistant at Metropolitan Interdenominational Church and the project coordinator says, "We are focusing on forgiveness because it is an integral struggle for those who have experienced sexual violence. It is difficult to tell someone who has been raised to believe that forgiveness is part of the Christian life that s/he doesn't have to forgive. Yet it is also problematic to insist that someone simply forgive immediately after a traumatic event. We want to be able to wrestle with this issue together in a church setting."

The first worship service, on [date], focused on community recognition. The remaining service will focus on healing.

The Dinah Project will provide educational workshops for clergy and laity to promote the awareness and appropriate response to the crisis of sexual violence in the community. The project will also coordinate counseling services designed to address the spiritual and theological issues for the victims, perpetrators, and the communities that love them.

By refusing to perpetuate the silence associated with incest, child sexual abuse, sexual assault, and rape, The Dinah Project hopes to address the spiritual and theological crises of sexual violence that few professionals currently provide.

Service of Healing Press Release

For Immediate Release
The Dinah Project—Sunday, [date]—5:00 P.M.
Ministry through the Arts
The Church Responds to Sexual Violence
[name of church]
[address]

[city, state]: Not your traditional church service! Used to a gospel choir and an invited preacher? Not this time! The Dinah Project of [name of church] brings worship and ministry through the performing and visual arts. Focusing on community awareness, we dare to talk about rape, sexual assault, and incest in the church.

Don't miss the storytelling craft of [name] or the well-known poetics of [another name]. On the floor, we will have original choreography by [name] and a special dance by [name], to an original composition written by [name].

The lineup includes the dramatic talent of [name], and performances by the hip-hop soul alternative [name]. The event would be incomplete without a few selections from the local choir and recording artists, [church choir]. Anticipate meditations from [pastor's name], and [advisory board member]. Feel free to bring children, as there will be structured activities for them as well. Like we said, not your traditional worship service!

Come see some of [name of your city]'s most talented artists come together to minister about sexual violence in the community. The service will start at 5 P.M. and admission is free. Make sure to pass this on.

The Dinah Project provides educational workshops for clergy and laity to promote the awareness and appropriate response to the crisis of sexual violence in the community. The project also coordinates counseling services designed to address the spiritual and theological issues for the victims, perpetrators, and the communities that love them. By refusing to perpetuate the silence associated with incest, child sexual abuse, sexual assault, and rape, The Dinah Project hopes to address the spiritual and theological crises of sexual violence that few professionals currently provide.

Contact: [project coordinator name] at [phone number] or [e-mail address] for additional information.

LETTER TO WORSHIP SERVICE PARTICIPANTS

[date]

Dear Dinah Project participant:

We here at [church name] are excited about your participation in The Dinah Project. For months, we have been praying for this ministry's growth and success. We are elated about your willingness and support in this first worship service on [date of service].

I have enclosed an early copy of the program. You should see the places where you will be fitting in. You will have approximately _____ minutes on the program.

I am asking all participants to be at the church by [thirty minutes before service starts]. This will ensure a good parking place and time to tie up any loose ends or answer questions that remain. This will also give you a chance to meet the other participants and helpers. Please be sure to pick up your white ribbon pin that will identify you as a helper and program participant.

If you have any additional questions, feel free to contact me at home, [phone number], or at [church name], [church phone number].

With Jesus' joy,
[name]
The Dinah Project coordinator

ORDERS OF WORSHIP

Community Awareness Service

The Gathering
Layers: A Dramatization
Meditation
Testimony
Solo
Introduction of Speaker
Preparatory Period—Music
The Message
Invitation to New Life
The Eucharist
Fellowship Circle
Litany of Affirmation

Service of Forgiveness

The Gathering
Affirmation of Faith
Skit—*Through the Glass*
Musical Selection
A Celebration of Solidarity
Introduction of Speaker
Preparatory Period—Music
The Message
Invitation to New Life
Fellowship Circle

Service of Healing

Invocation
Affirmation of Faith
Meditation
Testimony
Solo
Celebration in Song
Introduction of Speaker
Preparatory Period—Music
The Message
Invitation to New Life
Fellowship Circle

LITANIES

Litany of Affirmation

by Julia Emily Louisa Peebles

LEADER: We trust that beyond the absence

PEOPLE: There is presence;

LEADER : That beyond the pain

PEOPLE : There can be healing;

LEADER : That beyond the brokenness

PEOPLE : There can be wholeness;

LEADER : That beyond the hurting

PEOPLE : There may be forgiveness;

LEADER : That beyond the silence

PEOPLE : There may be the word;

LEADER : That through the word,

PEOPLE : There may be understanding;

ALL: *That through understanding, there is love.*

Litany of the Word

by Mary Pellauer

RIGHT: I was hungry and you gave me bread.

LEFT: I was thirsty and you gave me drink.

RIGHT: I was a stranger and you welcomed me.

LEFT: I was naked and you clothed me.

RIGHT: I was sick and you visited me.

LEFT: I was in prison and you came to me.

RIGHT: I was raped and you stood by me.

LEFT: I was beaten and you sheltered me.

RIGHT: I was harassed and you helped me act.

LEFT: I was abused and you intervened.

RIGHT: I was in pain and you comforted me.

LEFT: I was bleeding and you staunched my wound.

RIGHT: I was orphaned and you mothered me.

LEFT: I was alone and you took my hand.

RIGHT: I was unworthy and you believed in me.

LEFT: I was victimized and you empowered me.

RIGHT: I was confused and you brought insight.

LEFT: I was silent and you listened to me.

RIGHT: I was seeking and you searched with me.

LEFT: I was knocking and you opened the door.

A Celebration of Solidarity

by Mary Pellauer

LEADER: In the name of God who created and is creating, who redeemed and is redeeming, who sanctified and is sanctifying, us and the whole world,

PEOPLE: Amen.

LEADER: We confess that by our thoughts, words, and deeds, we have turned away from life; we have limited ourselves to meager life; we have chosen many small deaths.

PEOPLE: Forgive us, Lord.

LEADER: We confess that we have offered our sisters and brothers stones when they asked for bread; we have looked away from the needy; we have given death instead of life.

PEOPLE: Forgive us, Lord.

LEADER: We confess that we have not lived in the Source of Life; we have not believed in the Word of Life; we have not had the Spirit of Life.

PEOPLE: Forgive us, Lord.

LEADER: Jesus said, "Courage, your faith has made you whole. Go in peace and be healed." Again in other healing stories, Jesus said, "Your sins are forgiven."

ALL: *As our sin has been forgiven and we have been made whole, let us praise and celebrate that abundant life that was promised us, which we claim for our own and for the whole community of God's people. Amen.*

A DRAMATIZATION: *Through the Glass*

Through the Glass is a dramatic portrayal of an encounter between a man who has been charged (and imprisoned) with date rape, and the ex-girlfriend who accuses him. She struggles with her feelings about his actions and her ability to forgive him. The mother of the accused man also dialogues with him about what has happened. All this conversation occurs "through the glass" of the visitation room of a prison.

The dramatization portrays the anguish over the pressure to forgive. It shows the anger and the issues of forgiveness that arise in situations of sexual violence—especially when the assailant is an acquaintance. The mother's statements to her son that "it will take time" and we must "put it in the Lord's hands" support a view that the forgiveness process cannot be rushed, no matter how sincere the desire of the perpetrator. The role of the mother in this dramatization reminds worshippers that sexual violence is not a sin relegated to the individuals involved in the actual crime, but that it affects loved ones, like parents. The victim's act of prayer is just one example of the way in which the entire *Dinah Project* insists that we cannot abandon God.

Through the Glass
Written by Cynthia Turner-Graham, Monica A. Coleman, and Elliott Robinson.

WOMAN: I don't understand why you would do me this way. I told you that I didn't want to, and if you respected me, then you wouldn't have done what you did.

MAN: But baby, I thought you wanted to. You never refused me like that before in the whole nine months we've been together. I thought you were just playing. Please forgive me. I'm sorry.

WOMAN: I don't care if you're sorry! What you did was totally wrong! I said no, and I meant no. There was no reason for you to do what you did. I don't care if you were drunk or whatever was wrong with you. I said no, and I meant what I said.

MAN: Please understand that I didn't meant to hurt you, baby. Can't we just forget about this little misunderstanding and move on from here? We've got a chance to create something special.

WOMAN: How are we supposed to move on from here? I mean, you raped me, for God's sake! I refused your wishes and you just took what you wanted, like some . . . like some . . . animal!! There's no way we can move on from here. You know, it was my parents that made me press charges against you.

MAN: Oh, that figures. Why'd you have to go and tell them anyway? You know they never cared much for me. Please drop the charges, baby. Don't send me to the pen. You know I didn't meant to hurt you. I . . . I love you, baby. You're my girl! And I know you love me, too. You've just gotta accept my apology!

WOMAN: I had to tell my parents because I felt like I didn't have anywhere else to turn. Now, you know I really do want to accept your apology, but the more I think about it, the madder I get. If you really loved me like you say you do, you never would have violated me that way. Especially if you consider me your girl. Every time you do something to upset me, you say the same ol' stuff. That's why it's really hard for me to believe you this time. What makes this apology so different from all the others, huh?

MAN: Sure, I've done some things wrong, but now I can see the error of my ways. I understand how serious this was, and what it all means to you, and I can make it up to you if you let me, baby. You know how much I love you.

WOMAN: Yeah, I know. I've got your love all upside my head, and I'm still hurting down there from what you did. I don't know yet whether I'm gonna press charges. I'll have to think long and hard about that. But I do know one thing. Right now, it is very hard to find it within myself to forgive you. I want to believe that you really didn't mean to hurt me. But that does not excuse what you did to me, and I'm gonna have to do some serious thinking about this whole thing. I've got to go.

MAN: Baby! Baby, don't leave now! Don't leave me! I love you, baby! I didn't mean any harm!

WOMAN: I can't stand to look at you for another second! [Storms out]

MAN: Mama, I don't see what I did that was so wrong. She said she wanted to be my girlfriend, for crying out loud! She acted like she didn't want to do anything, but her body language was saying something totally different! I was sure that deep down, she really wanted to give it to me. She never refused me before. I swear I didn't mean to hurt her.

MOTHER: Now, son, you ought to know by now that just because you think she acted like she "wanted some," that doesn't mean a thing. You have to go by what she says. That's all you can go by. If she says no, then that is what she means. I thought you would have learned your lesson the last time, when that other girl didn't press charges on you, because she was too afraid of anybody finding out. Now I understand that you mean it when you say that you didn't mean to hurt her, and I'm willing to forgive you for what you've done.

MAN: Thank you, Mama, I knew you would understand. But what do I do now?

MOTHER: First of all, you ought to pray to the Lord for forgiveness. I heard that child ranting and raving all the way out here while I was waiting and she stormed past me crying something terrible. It will be easier to be forgiven by God than it will to be forgiven by that girl. She's very upset, son.

MAN: But I explained the whole thing to her, how I didn't meant to hurt her, and how much I love her and everything. But she's still upset.

MOTHER: Of course she's upset, son. What you did was very, very wrong. My prayer is that she will one day forgive you, and that we will all be able to pick up the pieces and move on. But just because I'm willing to give you another chance doesn't mean that she is.

MAN: But how can I make her understand? What can I do to get her to believe me?

MOTHER: That's something over which you have no control, son. Now you know I'll be praying, and I'm sure that there is a lesson to be learned here. I can only continue to pray, and hope that she will find forgiveness in her heart. I think that this lesson is one that you had to learn; I just hope you don't have a long prison sentence to study it over.

MAN: I understand what you're saying, Mama. But do you think there is any possible way I can make her understand?

MOTHER: No. There's nothing else you can do, son. You told her how you feel, and she told you how she feels. All you can do now is leave it in God's hands, and hope that the Holy Spirit will touch her in a way that allows her to find forgiveness in her heart, hardened as it may be toward you right now. It'll take some time. It'll take some time.

MAN: I'm scared Mama. I'm really scared.

MOTHER: C'mon now, son, and let's pray . . .

[both bow their heads, their hands pressed against the glass and the lights dim]

[*From off stage, you hear the woman's voice*]

Lord, you said you wouldn't leave me, and you said you wouldn't forsake me, but I'm feeling pretty alone right now. I mean, you know I refused him because I decided that we were going to do this thing right. Because I know that we've been going about this the wrong way. I mean, sex had become . . . it had become too important and I wanted for once to do it the right way, you know, Your way, you know, no sex before marriage. I have made some mistakes, I know that. I was trying to do the right thing, that time, and look what happened! I'm just so confused. I don't know what to do. I know my Grandmama says that God's grace is sufficient in every situation, no matter what happens, I can always depend on You. I know I have an angel. I've done some stupid things, look at where I am right now. You've got me out of some bad situations, you've picked me up and forgiven me and shown me how to do things the right way. I'm pretty hard-headed, huh? I guess there's supposed to be a place in my heart to forgive, but I don't feel like it. I can't see how I'm supposed to do it. I want to be able to forgive him, but I don't want to put myself in this situation again. I don't want something like this to happen all over again to me. And I know that your grace is sufficient. I know that. But . . . it's not that easy. How do I cope? I need you to help me out here. C'mon, help me out, God.

VOICES ON FORGIVENESS

Parts: Speaker A, Speaker B, Speaker C, Speaker D, and Person-in-Conflict

The Person-in-Conflict sits in the front of the room nonverbally responding in turmoil to the various messages being told about forgiveness. The voices of Speaker A, B, C, and D come from the different corners of the room (with microphones) as they tell the Person-in-Conflict different things about forgiveness. As Speaker A reads the last statement, Speakers B, C, and D can move toward the Person-in-Conflict to embrace that person.

SPEAKER A:
Our Father who art in heaven
Hallowed be thy name.
Thy kingdom come, thy will be done
On earth as it is in heaven.
Give us this day our daily bread
And forgive us our trespasses
As we forgive those who trespass against us.

SPEAKER B:
And forgive us our trespasses
As we forgive those who trespass against us.

SPEAKER C:
If you forgive others, God will also forgive you. But if you do not forgive others, neither will God forgive you.

SPEAKER D:
How often can someone sin against me; how often must I forgive them? Seven times?

SPEAKER B:
No. Up to seventy times seven.

SPEAKER C:
Whenever you pray, if you have anything against anyone, forgive them.

SPEAKER D:
If someone sins against you, rebuke them.

SPEAKER B:
If someone repents, forgive them. If they sin against you seven times in the day and turn to you seven times and say, "I repent," you must forgive them.

SPEAKER C:
Forgive and forget; there's nothing you can do about it now.

SPEAKER D:
But how can I ever forget?

SPEAKER B:
Isn't it time you forgave? If God can forgive, surely you can too.

SPEAKER C:
Which is easier? To tell a paralyzed person to get up and walk or to say to someone: "Your sins are forgiven."

SPEAKER D:
You don't have to forgive. Just focus on yourself and your own healing.

SPEAKER A:
We do not have to know how to forgive. All we have to do is be willing to forgive. God will take care of the how. When the word "forgiving" is mentioned, who comes to your mind? Who is the person or what is the experience that you feel you will never forget, never forgive? What is it that holds you to the past? When you refuse to forgive, you hold onto the past, and it is impossible for you to be in the present. It is only when you are in the present that you can create your future. Forgiving is a gift to yourself. It frees you from the past, the past experience and past relationships. It allows you to live in present time. When you forgive yourself and forgive others, you are indeed free. There is a tremendous sense of freedom that comes with forgiveness. Often you need to forgive yourself for putting up with painful experiences and not loving yourself enough to move away from those experiences. So love yourself. Forgive yourself, forgive others, and be in the moment. See the old bitterness and the old pain just roll off your shoulders as you let go. And let the doors of your heart open wide. When you come from a space of love you are always safe. Forgive everyone. Forgive yourself. Forgive all past experiences. You are free.

TESTIMONIES

David's Story: I Wrestled

I'm a little nervous. Disappointment. Helplessness. Abandonment. Fear. Shame. I wrestle with that. Not because of choice. Because of chance. It happened to me. It's my story. It's a part of who I am as a man. I look normal, but I wrestle. From seven to the age of eleven, I wrestled. In the arms of another man, I wrestled. Names that were foreign to me. I wrestled. Touch. The smell. The invasion. The phone calls. The threats. I wrestled. After school play. I wrestled. Lying to my mother. I wrestled. Quiet. Shy. Begin stuttering at age eight. I wrestled. No longer playing as a child. No more softball. No more bicycle riding. I wrestled. Lying to my mother. I wrestled. Became an A student in school because I thought that would fix it. I wrestled. Took showers after showers after showers. God knows I wrestled. Grew up as a teenager not knowing who I am, couldn't voice it. It silenced me. I wrestled. Went off to college. No stable relationships. Distrust. Not able to form any type of community at school. I wrestled.

One day, I heard in the community of Memphis about a place where people like me could go. And I called my cousin and I shared with her. She said, "Call them." And I paced the floor with phone in hand, and I dialed the number. And they answered and said, "Christian Counseling Center. How may I help you? How may I direct your call?" And the first thing I said was, "I need help." And they said, "What's the problem?" And I said " I can't tell you over the phone. Who do I need to talk to?" And that moment changed my life. And I entered the Center not knowing what was going to happen. But I knew I wanted a change. And you know what, I didn't even pray to God about it; I just walked through the doors. Because God and I were not on speaking terms. I was angry. Why me? Was it my walk? Was it the way I talk? There's three boys in my family. Why me? And I remember session after session struggling with it, trying to say the words. And it happened one day. I whispered it. And I said, "I was raped." And that started the healing.

I joined a men's group: New Creations, in Memphis. I will never forget it and it revolutionized my life. It was nine months into the group that I shed my first tear. It was a long process. And I remember what the facilitator told me. He said, "You have just now begun to deal." And I have been dealing ever since. I'm trusting better. I have better relationships now. I'm beginning to love me. I touch my own body now. It's a good thing. And it's healthy. Because for many years, it didn't belong to me. So

I own who I am. And it's all because of an outreach center through a church. Through an African American church in Memphis. Because we don't talk about this. It's a silent issue. And we as men sho nuff don't talk about it. You must be gay. You must be a queer. You were in the arms of another man for all those years. What did you do? All those "isms" and myths. But God told me one day in the bathroom. This is the healing. This is the process for me. Just a normal shower, a normal day for me. And I stepped out of the shower and there was a full-length mirror in the bathroom and God says, "You are fearfully and wonderfully made." And it was the first time that I looked at myself. I normally would rush by the mirror. But I stopped this time and God said, "Touch everything that's on you. It's blessed. It's ordained. It's perfect. It's good. It's yours." And I stayed in that bathroom, wet and cold, for a long time. I couldn't get dressed, but I stayed because it was the first time in my life that I enjoyed my own nakedness. Shame, disappointment, fear, silence. I wrestled!

Now I stand as a person in recovery. It invades my privacy every now and again. But I check it. It intrudes on the calmness of my mind, my spirit. But I check it! I no longer measure myself by American standards anymore. For I am unique. For I am different. For I am David. For many years, I was *his* boy, *his* toy, *his* plaything. "Don't you tell." "I'm going to kill you." "Your parents are going to put you in a home." "No one wants you." "I'm all you got." And I heard my name. David. And I own it. And it's mine. And I am who God says I am. So there are brothers out there who are like me. And I hope that this forum and this church will swing the doors open so that we can heal. So that we can mourn. So that we can recollect ourselves. So that we can go back and take what was wrongfully stolen from us. I used to wrestle. But I wrestled!

Leah's Story: A Letter to My Abusers

I am still here, healthy and free. I know you are surprised. According to the experts, a girl who has been through what you put me through is not supposed to be sane. You see, I was supposed to be destroyed. But I am still here. Right now, I am supposed to be in and out of rehab centers or suffering from low self-esteem. But I am not. I am supposed to be degrading myself in a strip club or in someone's porno movie, but I am not. I am supposed to be so depressed that I drop out of school, of life, but I have not. I am supposed to go through life thinking it was my fault that somehow I made a four-, eight- and ten-year-old body too enticing or that I was so worthless and low that I caused people to want to abuse me. But I do not. And I know not. I am supposed to be unable to be in a healthy relationship and I am supposed to think that sex is dirty and disgusting, but I don't and I have healthy friendships and healthy relationships.

You did not break me. I didn't just survive. I am living. And when I become a doctor, I will help little girls and little boys whose innocence has been taken. I will report every time I suspect sexual abuse and I will testify in a court of law. I will tell them that they are beautiful and I will hold them in my arms and tell them that it will be all right. I will teach how to tell and to run when they can. I will show them that they are special and I will tell them it is not their fault over and over again until they believe it. I will counsel them and show them how to live. I will bring a spotlight and shine it in the face of every abuser until this country speaks out loud and addresses this the way they address heart disease. And I give you this warning: You always get what you give out. I hope to God it does not come back to you through the children. Not for your sake, but for theirs.

Appendix D

Go Tell It on the Mountain— Community Education Resources

SEXUAL VIOLENCE QUESTIONNAIRE

Circle T (true) or F (false).

T F 1. Sexual violence is almost exclusively an inner city phenomenon.

T F 2. Sexual offenders are usually men deprived of sexual relations.

T F 3. Children cannot be sexually violated.

T F 4. Only women can be raped.

T F 5. If there is no weapon or actual physical violence, a woman cannot bring charges of sexual assault.

T F 6. Men cannot be sexually violated.

T F 7. It is common for more than a year to pass before a rape case comes to trial.

T F 8. Women who hitchhike or go alone to bars are asking to be raped or sexually assaulted.

T F 9. A wife cannot be raped by her husband.

T   F   10. Immediately after a sexual violation, some victims are very composed and calm.

T   F   11. Hospitals will automatically notify the police and the victim's family.

T   F   12. In the majority of sexual violence cases, the victim and assailant are of different races.

T   F   13. Being raped ruins the victim's future sexual adjustment.

T   F   14. Many rapes would be eliminated if women would not dress seductively.

T   F   15. In order to press charges, the victim must hire an attorney.

T   F   16. Testimony about a victim's past sexual conduct is important evidence in a rape trial.

T   F   17. Most victims who are raped blame themselves.

T   F   18. Many victims do not tell their spouses, parents, or family members that they were sexually violated.

T   F   19. It is unnecessary for a victim to go to a hospital unless there is physical injury.

T   F   20. Most victims do not know their victimizers.

T   F   21. Most incidents of sexual violence are reported to the police.

T   F   22. Most incidents of sexual violence happen on the streets.

T   F   23. Sexual violence is the most underreported violent crime in the United States.

T   F   24. Over 50 percent of all incidents of sexual violence occur between people who have met before.

T   F   25. A major problem in investigating cases of sexual violence is that people frequently make false accusations.

T   F   26. Since many women have rape fantasies, it is possible that women enjoy being raped.

T   F   27. Sexual violence is an expression of hostility, aggression, and dominance.

OTHER QUESTIONNAIRES ABOUT SEXUAL VIOLENCE

http://www.justicewomen.com/cj_rapequiz_en.html

http://www.netstuff.com/target/rape.htm

http://www.acar.org/quiz/

http://www.clevelandrapecrisis.org/forms/EducationQuiz.asp?return=default.asp?c=1005

http://www.gwu.edu/~cade/quiz.htm

http://www.coolnurse.com/rape_active_quiz.htm

QUIZ ABOUT CHILD SEXUAL ABUSE

http://www.smith-lawfirm.com/Connsacs_Myth_Quiz.htm

DEFINITIONS OF SEXUAL VIOLENCE

Sexual abuse: Nonconsensual sexual relations

Sexual assault: Nonconsensual sexual violation including rape and such nonpenetrating acts as touching, groping, undressing, sucking

Rape: Penetration with a penis, finger, or other foreign object

Acquaintance rape: Rape by someone known

Stranger rape: Rape by someone unknown

Date rape: Rape by someone with whom there is an ongoing relationship

Gang rape: Rape by two or more persons

Marital rape: Rape by a spouse

Incest: Sexual assault or rape by a family member

Child sexual abuse: Sexual assault or rape of anyone under eighteen

Unequal power dimensions: Sexual relations, even if they are consensual, between persons of unequal power or status. Examples include relationships of teacher/student, employer/employee, counselor/ client, doctor/patient, attorney/client, minister/parishioner, and persons of different military rank.

STATISTICS

Updated statistics can be found at www.rainn.org.

A total of 17.7 million women have been victims of a rape or sexual assault (*Prevalence, Incidence and Consequences of Violence Against Women Survey*, National Institute of Justice and Centers for Disease Control and Prevention, 1998).

Approximately 48 percent of victims are raped by a friend or acquaintance, 30 percent by a stranger, 16 percent by an intimate partner, and 2 percent by other relatives (*2000 National Crime Victimization Survey*, Bureau of Justice Statistics, U.S. Department of Justice).

Only 39 percent of all rapes are reported to the police (*1999 National Crime Victimization Survey*, Bureau of Justice Statistics, U.S. Department of Justice).

An overwhelming majority of rape service agencies believe that public education about rape, and expanded counseling and advocacy services for rape victims, would be effective in increasing the willingness of victims to report rapes to the police (*Rape in America*, National Victim Center with Crime Victims Research and Treatment Center, 1992).

Only one of every twelve rapes takes place in a public area or in a parking garage (*Sex Offenses and Offenders*, Bureau of Justice Statistics, U.S. Department of Justice, 1997).

A total of 67 percent of rapes occur between the hours of 6 P.M. and 6 A.M. (*Sex Offenses and Offenders*, Bureau of Justice Statistics, U.S. Department of Justice, 1997).

In 2001, only about 7 percent of rapes involve the use of a weapon (*2000 National Crime Victimization Survey*, Bureau of Justice Statistics, U.S. Department of Justice).

A total of 2.78 million men have experienced an attempted or completed rape in their lifetime (*Prevalence, Incidence and Consequences of Violence Against Women*, National Institute of Justice and Centers for Disease Control and Prevention, 1998).

44 percent of rape victims are under age eighteen; 15 percent are under age twelve (*Sex Offenses and Offenders*, Bureau of Justice Statistics, U.S. Department of Justice, 1997).

Nearly 30 percent of all juvenile victims of sexual abuse cases are children between ages four and seven (*Child Maltreatment*, U.S. Department of Health and Human Services, Administration for Children and Families, 1995).

As many as 3 percent of boys in grades five through eight and 5 percent of boys in grades nine through twelve said they had been sexually abused (*Commonwealth Fund Survey of the Health of Adolescent Boys*, 1998).

In one study, 98 percent of males who raped boys reported that they were heterosexual ("Sexual Abuse of Boys," *Journal of the American Medical Association*, December 2, 1998).

Girls ages sixteen to nineteen are four times more likely than the general population to be victims of rape, attempted rape, or sexual assault (*2000 National Crime Victimization Survey*, Bureau of Justice Statistics, U.S. Department of Justice).

Among people ages twelve and older, about 82.5 percent of rape victims are white; 13.3 percent are black; only 4.2 percent of assaults are interracial (*2000 National Crime Victimization Survey*, Bureau of Justice Statistics, U.S. Department of Justice).

RESPONSES TO SEXUAL VIOLENCE
Popular Ineffective Responses

Look at you. What happened to you?

What were you doing in that neighborhood? Don't you know that bad people hang out there?

Your mother was right. You shouldn't have fought back. You should have known better.

This would never happen to me. I wouldn't get into such a situation.

How old were the men who robbed you? It's terrible—they should be working.

What can you expect from that kind of person?

I expect more of you. Why did you get in such a mess? Can't you take care of yourself?

Of course you should prosecute—are you going to just let them walk free?

It's your own fault.

What happened? When? Where?

You're so upset; you need a shrink!

I'm trying to help. Let me help you.

You need to stop dwelling on what happened. Think about something else.

Maybe your whole family needs counseling.

You aren't listening to me.

You are right not to prosecute. Why upset yourself? Try to get over this quickly.

It's so hard to see you so upset. What can I do to make you feel better?

If only you'd listen to me, I'm sure we can solve your problems.

What happened? Oh that sounds horrible.

My God, what did you do then? I couldn't have stood it; I would've collapsed right there.

What are you going to do?

Prosecute? What's the use? The judge will just let him off. It takes forever.

I wish you weren't so upset.

I'm beginning to feel sick.

Isn't it terrible, what the world is coming to? What are we going to do?

This is too much for me to handle.

Effective responses

What happened? You really had a tough time.

I can understand how upset you feel.

It would be hard to sleep after an experience like that.

Tell me more, if you like.

It's frightening to think you might have been hurt worse or killed.

I'm glad you are alive.

It takes time to get over such difficult feelings.

You really handled the situation well.

It must be hard for you to be upset when your family is upset too.

It seems like you're feeling upset and kind of alone in all this.

It's hard when your family doesn't seem to understand how you feel.

You're having trouble deciding whether to prosecute? What are your thoughts?

You seem worried that you fought back when you were attacked. It's true that it did put you in a difficult situation, but I wonder if it also feels good to you that you didn't just "take it."

It's getting late and I have to leave soon. Do you want to let me know how you feel tomorrow? Would you like me to call you?

LAYERS: A Dramatization

This exercise is inspired by a similar orchestrated drama in Marie Fortune's *Violence in Families: A Workshop Curriculum For Clergy and Other Helpers.* An adult sits in a chair. On the ground nearby are seven white sheets. Fourteen persons are selected from the congregation shortly before the service begins and given a sheet of paper with a statement on it. On the reverse side of the paper are the words "Put Sheet On" or "Take Sheet Off." When a person hears "his/her line," s/he gets up from his/her seat (dispersed around the building) and either places a sheet on top of the person in the chair, or takes a sheet off.

A worship leader reads the lines before each person places or removes a sheet. The lines for the seven people who place sheets on the person in the chair are as follows:

1. Don't tell anyone. No one will ever believe you.
2. I'm a six-year-old boy whose babysitter made me touch her private parts.
3. God let this happen to you for a reason.
4. No one else could possibly understand what I'm going through.
5. When I told my mother what my stepfather did, she said it was my fault.
6. It wouldn't have happened to you if you didn't wear those skimpy dresses.
7. What did you do to make him think you wanted it?

The lines for the seven people who remove sheets from the person in the chair are:

1. It's okay to be mad at and question God.
2. I believe you.
3. God loves you and I love you too.
4. It wasn't your fault that this happened to you.
5. I'm here to listen . . . whenever.
6. God hears your cries.
7. We will get through this together.

This dramatization intends to reveal the situations and suffering of those who have experienced sexual violence. By providing scenarios of abuse and statements that perpetuate silence and abuse, persons can visually understand the way in which sexual violence, and society's silence and theology, alienates a victim under layers and layers of pain and isolation. The images that correspond to the removing of the sheets demonstrate the ways in which certain statements, theologies, and empathetic words can restore the victim to community. This exercise also serves as a teaching moment for those who have not experienced sexual violence to know words that are oppressive or liberating to say to someone who has chosen to break the silence that too often follows sexual violence.

GOALS AND OBJECTIVES FOR COMMUNITY EDUCATION SESSIONS
For Clergy

Attention all rape victims: don't go to church! In most areas of the country, there are medical, psychological, and legal resources for victims of sexual violence. But there are no spiritual resources to help victims of sexual violence with the healing process that affects all aspects of their lives. In fact, the church's silence surrounding issues of sexual violence and sexuality in general makes the church's position, at best, ambiguous and, at worst, condemning and shaming. By perpetuating this silence and ignoring the way in which sexual violence pervades our biblical and sociological realities, the church has become the last place one should go in a crisis of the experience of sexual violence.

This workshop challenges us to seriously examine biblical and theological perspectives on sexual violence. What does the Bible have to say about rape and incest? How can we enter into dialogue with these passages? What important theological issues are raised in the crisis of the experience of sexual violence? How should victims respond? How should we deal with violators? What can loved ones do?

- Be sure the environment that a victim encounters in churches is open and compassionate.
- Examine what the Bible has to say.
- Raise the theological issues involved in sexual violence.

This workshop will also provide some tangible ways local churches can address sexual violence in a communal setting. How can we help to create a safe place for discussion of the issue? How can we partner with other resources in the community? How can we provide a resource that other agencies in the community do not provide? How can we talk about sexual violence during worship or Christian education settings?

- Become educated about the issue.
- Monitor interpersonal responses.
- Develop relationships with other service providers in the community.
- Establish programmatic efforts in our churches.

What Clergy Can Do

- Preach and teach on biblical passages dealing with intimate violence.
- Refer, refer, refer.
- Learn the difference between helpful and unhelpful things to say.

Do not say:

- "God let this happen for a reason."
- "All things work together for the good of those who love the Lord."
- "What did you do to cause . . . ?"

For Service Providers

What can I do? Addressing the spiritual in sexual abuse: In most areas of the country, there are medical, psychological, and legal resources for persons dealing with the crises of suicide, domestic violence, and sexual violence. But there are no spiritual resources to help victims or loved ones with the healing process that affects all aspects of their lives. In fact, the church's silence surrounding issues of violence and intimate and personal violence, in particular, makes the church's position, at best, ambiguous and, at worst, condemning and shaming. By perpetuating this silence and ignoring the way in which intimate violence pervades our biblical, theological, and sociological realities, the church has become the last place one should go in a crisis of the experience of intimate violence. As a result, nonclergy service providers have had to pick up the slack in giving spiritual guidance to those in these types of crisis. Many providers feel ill equipped to handle these issues that produce a spiritual and cognitive dissonance within clients as they try to reconcile their experiences, emotions, and the teaching of their religious upbringings.

This workshop is designed to offer service providers information on some of the spiritual dimensions of intimate violence. What theological issues are raised in the context of intimate violence? What resources do most clergy have? What issues are beyond their expertise? Which issues are within their purview of care and counsel? How can nonclergy address some of these spiritual issues?

What Service Providers Can Do

- Meet with local clergy to tell them about the services you provide. Develop a referral relationship.
- Leave brochures about your services in an accessible place in local churches (such as inside bathrooms).
- Emphasize God's presence, God's love, and God's grace.
- Emphasize biblical traditions of giving every emotion to God, and Jesus' own display of emotion. Some examples can be found in Psalm 55 (experience), Psalm 38 (confusion), Psalm 88 (unrelieved depression), Psalm 94 (righteous anger), Psalm 121 (comfort), Psalm 124 (survivors); Mark 14:32–42, Matthew 26:36–46, John 2:13–22.
- Don't rush the client to reconcile spiritual issues immediately.
- Divorce the concepts of forgetting, denial, forgiveness, reconciliation, and salvation and connect concepts of the body and the spirit.

BIBLICAL EXPLORATION ABOUT SEXUAL VIOLENCE

One way to explore what the Bible says about sexual violence is to ask workshop participants to briefly study biblical passages that complicate our understanding of sexual violence. For each workshop, we print out copies of the following questions and attach them to the printed passages.

Passages Used

Narrative passages (Bible stories):
    The rape of Dinah: Genesis 34
    The Levite's concubine: Judges 19
    The rape of Tamar: 2 Samuel 13
    David and Bathsheba: 2 Samuel 11

Nonnarrative passages (epistles, laws, and wisdom):
    Ephesians 5:22–6:9

Reflections on Narrative Biblical Passages

Who are the characters?

Who are the victim(s) and who are the victimizer(s)?

Who are the witnesses, bystanders, or other players, if any?

What does the community do in response to this violence?

Based on this story, what are some communal/family consequences of this violence?

How does the victimizer use/abuse power?

What do we learn about this victim from this story?

What do we learn about the victimizer from this story?

What are some positive teachings from this passage, if any?

What are some negative things learned from this passage, if any?

What does this tell us about how God feels about sexual violence?

Reflections on Nonnarrative Biblical Passages

Who has/is given power in this passage?

How can this power be abused?

What does this passage tell us about how power and authority should be exercised?

How might this passage be helpful in family dynamics?

How might this passage be problematic in family dynamics?

What are some positive teachings from this passage, if any?

What are some negative things learned from this passage, if any?

What does this tell us about how God feels about sexual violence?

Reflection on Testimony

If you used excerpts from testimonies or from services or decide to read/perform testimonies found in books or on the Internet, use these reflection questions to begin to open discussion on theological issues.

What emotions does the victim feel in the experience of and recovery from sexual violence?

Which of those emotions are specifically theological or affect the relationship with God?

Weep with Those Who Weep— Forms for Group Counseling

VOLUNTEER SIGN-UP

VOLUNTEER OPPORTUNITIES

Child care 6:00–8:30 P.M. [day of meeting]
Meal preparation 5:45–6:45 P.M. [day of meeting]
Male presence/security 5:45–6:45 P.M. [day of meeting]
Administrative faxing and sending out press releases
Creative singing, dramatic presentation
Liturgical worship assistants during services

DINAH PROJECT VOLUNTEERS

Name	Phone Number	Activity

LETTER TO VOLUNTEERS

Thank you so much for volunteering to work with The Dinah Project. Your contribution is invaluable! As I mentioned when we spoke on the phone, this little note just gives me the opportunity to write out the details of some of the things to which you agreed.

You volunteered to assist with the Dinah Group. The Dinah Group is a twelve-week program for the healing of survivors of sexual abuse. The Dinah Groups meet every [insert day of the week] evening at [location], ([insert street address]) for the months of February, March, and April.

The Dinah Group ensures confidentiality for its clients. It is important to remember that *the day of the week, the location, and the identity of the clients is confidential* and should not be shared with anyone under any circumstances. I will ask you to sign a confidentiality statement agreeing to that when you appear to volunteer. I appreciate this effort because confidentiality is key to the success of the Dinah Groups.

Meal Preparation, 5:45–6:45 P.M. [day of meeting]

Dinah Group participants arrive between 6:00 and 6:30 P.M. Dinner should be ready at 6:00. Please stay long enough to collect leftovers and take them home with you!

- Please prepare a meal for seven individuals.
- Please prepare a beverage, two dishes, and something sweet to eat.
- (Plastic ware is already at the church).
- You may be reimbursed for up to $50.00 per meal cooked. Just keep the receipt and give it to [project coordinator's name] within the week. Please write your full name on the back of the receipt.

Child Care, 6:00–8:30 P.M. [day of meeting]

There will be space in [specific location] in the church to help with the child(ren).

Security, 5:45–6:45 P.M. [day of meeting]

Dinah Project participants use the [specific entrance] to the building. Since this entrance can be dark and daunting in the evening hours, we need men to be present and vigilant near the entrance. I will always try to have at least two or three men in the area. You can stand outside and talk, or sit in your cars if it is cold—although preferably in one car.

Persons doing meal preparation and security should be free in time for prayer meeting at 7:00 P.M. should you decide to attend.

If you have any questions, feel free to call me at [insert number]. Thanks again

[name]
project coordinator

SAMPLE FLIER/POSTER FOR DINAH GROUPS

YOUR
CHURCH
LOGO

As an adult or child, have you ever been:

- Touched in sexual areas without your permission?
- Forced to perform oral sex on an adult or sibling?
- Raped or molested by a relative or someone else you know?
- Fondled, kissed, or held in a way that made you uncomfortable?
- Made to watch sexual acts or look at sexual parts?
- Encouraged or goaded into sex you didn't really want?

And do you have difficulty:

- Expressing your sexuality?
- Setting boundaries in relationships?
- Going to church or praying again after the abuse?
- Trusting family and/or romantic partners?
- Healing from the pain?
- Managing your anger?

The Dinah Group may be right for you!

Introducing The Dinah Group

A free 12-week program for the healing of survivors of sexual violence

- Dealing with emotional issues resulting from your experience
- Addressing spiritual and biblical issues associated with rape and sexual assault

For more information, Call The Dinah Project at [phone number]

CONFIDENTIALITY AGREEMENT

I understand that my signature indicates my agreement to keep confidential all information about The Dinah Project clients and any statistics, research, information, or data derived from [name of crisis center] clients or programs (collectively, the "Dinah Project Information") and I understand that disclosing client information is an ethical and legal violation of the clients' rights.

I understand that permission must be obtained in writing from the executive director, program director, and client or clients involved before use of any Dinah Project Information.

I understand that any Dinah Project Information acquired as result of my past, present, and/or future affiliation with The Dinah Project is to be kept confidential pursuant to this agreement. I also understand that a violation of this agreement could result in my immediate dismissal from service with The Dinah Project. I agree that I will continue to keep [name of crisis center] confidential even after I am no longer affiliated with the [name of crisis center] and/or The Dinah Project.

My signature below indicates that I have read this agreement.

Signature _____

Date _____

Witness _____

Date _____

STATEMENT OF CONFIDENTIALITY

The client files and records are kept strictly confidential. They are stored in a secure location and are not accessible to anyone except the program director and the administrative assistant. Any funding agency and/or its designees, auditor and/or representatives, and pastoral staff shall agree to and sign the same.

The [name of crisis center] promises to never disclose any personal information including but not limited to: name, address, phone number, employment status, and disease progression information, to anyone without the expressed permission of the client. Any agency reporting uses client identification numbers only, and shall not discuss issues relative to the client that might give away a client's identity.

A client may review his/her personal file with the program director at any time.

In addition, no staff or volunteer will leave any client identifying or personal information in a message for a client at his/her home or place of employment. Any mail sent to the client will be delivered in nonidentifiable envelopes and is only sent at the request of the client to the address the client specifies.

I understand these policies as written and explained to me.

Client signature _____

Date _____

Agency representative _____

Date _____

GRIEVANCE POLICY

All recipients of services of The Dinah Project are entitled to participate in the activities of this organization without undue stress and conflict. Should a conflict or irreconcilable difference regarding confrontation occur with any employee or volunteer of The Dinah Project, clients are encouraged to take the following steps.

1. The client should verbally contact the program director and outline the grievance(s) in writing.
2. If the conflict occurs with the program director, the client should verbally contact the executive director and outline the grievance(s) in writing.

The employee, volunteer, or program director will be made aware of the client's grievance within twenty-four hours of the occurrence. Attempts at mediation will occur with the program director, the client, and the employee or volunteer involved. If the grievance is filed against the program director, the executive director will review the grievance and take the proper steps toward mediation.

If the client is dissatisfied with the outcome of the grievance, outside mediation is available through related agencies whose mission and goals are similar to those of The Dinah Project.

Every effort will be made to maintain confidentiality during the grievance period and thereafter.

Please note that verbal notification is sufficient to begin a review of the grievance or complaint.

All grievances should be addressed to:

[name]

[address]

[phone number]

AUTHORIZATION FOR RELEASE OF INFORMATION

Name: _____

Address: _____

_____

_____

Date of Birth: _____

Social Security No.: _____

I authorize release of the following information (check all that apply):

_____ Medical history, examination, laboratory test, and treatment reports

_____ Psychological test reports

_____ Psychiatric evaluation reports

_____ Social history data including family, education, employment, and other relevant material

_____ Summary of previous mental health treatment

_____ Periodic report of current treatment progress including attendance and participation

_____ Notification of referral source of initiation and termination

_____ Legal records (court orders, police reports, etc.)

_____ Other information (specify): _____

_____

From/to The Dinah Project

From/to (name of organization or individual): _____

_____

Address: _____

_____

_____

I understand that this information will be used for the following specific purpose (check all that apply):

_____ To develop a diagnosis, treatment, and rehabilitation plan

_____ To coordinate the medical, psychological, and social rehabilitation process

_____ Other use (specify): _____

_____

I understand no information may be redisclosed by either agency to any other individual or agency unless by my written consent.

This authorization may be revoked at any time by my written statement and it is automatically revoked at the end of ninety days or under the following specific conditions: _____

_____

_____

This consent for release of information is given freely, voluntarily, and without coercion.

Client signature _____

Date _____

Dinah Project counselor signature _____

Date _____

CLIENT INFORMATION

Client name: _____ Date: _____

Address: _____

_____

Phone numbers: Home _____ Work _____

Date of birth: _____ Race: _____

Social security number: _____

Emergency contact: _____

Relationship: _____ Phone: _____

Current counselor: _____

Can we contact your counselor? Yes _____ No _____

Address: _____

_____

Phone: _____ Fax: _____

List all people living in your household: _____

Name	Relation	Age

Marital status:_____ Since what date: _____

Previous primary relationships:

Name	Married?	Years together	Children	Ages

Are you currently in a primary relationship?_____ How long? _____

Does that person know you are attending this group?_____

Pending legal issues related to group treatment: _____

_____

_____

How have you been feeling in the past two weeks? (Circle one.)

miserable   unhappy   OK   happy   very happy

Please list ALL previous counseling/psychotherapy or psychiatric treatment. Please include any psychiatric hospitalizations or other inpatient treatment (alcohol and drug, eating disorders, codependency):

Name	Where	Why	Dates

Describe any past family history of:

Physical abuse: _____

_____

Sexual abuse: _____

_____

Drug/alcohol abuse: _____

_____

Suicide attempts: _____

_____

Psychiatric problems: _____

_____

Have you been or do you suspect that you may have been a victim of child physical, emotional, or sexual abuse/molestation or rape? Explain.

_____

_____

Have you always been aware of it or realized it? _____

_____

_____

Have you been a victim of rape as an adult? Explain. _____

_____

_____

During the past two years, have you experienced the following?

Deaths of family members/friends: _____

_____

Relocations: _____

_____

Other traumatic/stressful event(s): _____

_____

Please circle if you have noticed any recent physical changes: vision, hearing, coordination, balance, strength, speech, memory, thinking, energy, sleeping, eating, elimination, sexual interest,

other: _____

Explain: _____

_____

Have alcohol and drugs ever been a problem for you? Explain.

_____

_____

Do you suspect that you may be using some behavior in a compulsive and possibly destructive way? Explain. (Examples: food, shopping, sex, exercise, gambling, religion, work)

_____

_____

_____

Have you ever seriously considered suicide? _____

Have you ever talked to a therapist about it? _____

Highest level of education: _____

What do you do for fun or enjoyment? _____

_____

What would you like to do for fun that you are not currently doing?

_____

What is your greatest strength? _____

_____

Who or what is your greatest emotional support? _____

_____

What is your greatest source of hope? _____

_____

What part, if any, does religion/spirituality play in your life? _____

_____

_____

How has your life changed recently? _____

_____

What has prompted you to join this group? _____

_____

What do you hope to accomplish in therapy? _____

_____

_____

JOURNAL OF GROUP PROGRESS

Date: _____   Topic: _____

Notes: _____

_____

_____

_____

_____

_____

Therapist _____

Date: _____   Topic: _____

Notes: _____

_____

_____

_____

_____

Therapist _____

DINAH PROJECT GROUP NOTES PER CLIENT

Date: _____ Topic: _____

Client: _____

_____

Participation: ____ High   ____ Moderate   ____ Low

Responsiveness: ____ High   ____ Moderate   ____ Low

Attentiveness: ____ High   ____ Moderate   ____ Low

_____

Progress notes: _____

_____

_____

_____

_____

_____

_____

_____

_____

_____

_____

_____

_____

Therapist _____

Appendix F

Master Checklist

RESEARCH

Places to Gather Information

- Rape crisis center
- Police department
- Medical services
- Less obvious places

Questions to Ask

- Do you have literature I can take with me?
- What books or articles would you recommend that I read?
- Are your services free and open to the public?
- Are there other agencies or individuals in the community that also address this need?
- Are juvenile victims and violators treated any differently?

- What is your policy on confidentiality?
- (If this agency does not deal explicitly with sexual violence, ask:) What percentage of the populace you serve indicates experiences as a victim or violator of sexual violence?
- Are there any recurring spiritual issues that you hear in your work? Hoe you do address those?
- Do you have special professional or volunteer training that I can attend?
- Is there anyone in a speakers' bureau who might be willing to talk with me and answer questions?

SELF TRAINING

- Community organizations
- Print and Internet resources
- Conferences

Things You Can Do

- Educate yourself about sexual violence and the spiritual effects it has upon a community.
- Write an article in your church newsletter. Include phone numbers to call.
- Make additions to the church library with pamphlets and books.
- Attach pamphlets and flyers to the bulletin board.
- Put information about counseling services and crisis hotlines in discrete locations such as restrooms.
- Invite workers from local agencies to conduct brief workshops at your church.
- Invite members of the church to volunteer with local agencies.
- Donate money to nonprofit agencies working to respond to sexual violence in your community.
- Encourage a group of church members or a particular church organization to attend a rally or event that addresses sexual violence in your community (for example, Take Back the Night).

GETTING ORGANIZED
Look for Board Members Who:

- Enjoy research,
- Have grant-writing or budgeting skills,
- Have creative or dramatic skills,
- Demonstrate a commitment to health issues,
- Possess a background in social work or psychology,
- Work with children through education or juvenile justice work,
- Work with populations that may contain a high percentage of those who are victims or perpetrators of sexual violence.

The Task of the Committee

- Develop vision and mission statements.
- Design a logo or promotional materials.
- Conduct a needs assessment.
- Provide artistic or clinical support.
- Help to coordinate volunteers.
- Keep archives of the ministry.
- Seek funding for the ministry.

WORSHIP
Checklist for Organizing a Worship Service

- Choose a theme for the service.
- Identify a time and date for each service.
- Be traditional with a lot of creativity.
- Find a preacher.
- Remove barriers that might prevent people from coming.
- Provide aftercare for issues that arise.
- Use publicity effectively.
- Video-/audiotape the services.
- Develop a budget.
- Utilize volunteer activity.

Things Volunteers Can Do

- Fax press releases and deliver flyers and pictures.
- Design the flyer and worship guides/printed bulletin.
- Make follow-up calls to media and agency representatives.
- Act as agency representatives (if qualified) available for aftercare or children's activities.
- Provide childcare.
- Video-/audiotape the services.
- Be prayer partners for aftercare issues.
- Cater or prepare food for the repast.
- Distribute worship guides/printed programs during the event.
- Serve as ushers during the events.
- Provide transportation.

Evaluation

- Get an estimate of the number of attendees.
- Maintain records of events.
- Follow up with those requesting information.
- Gather a sampling of attendees to get their impressions of the event.
- Listen to the tapes of the service.

COMMUNITY EDUCATION

Handouts Should Include

- The goals and objectives of the session
- Church contact information
- Statistics on and definitions of sexual violence
- Popular effective and ineffective responses
- Bibliography

Topics to Include

- Find out where people are.
- Engage the tradition.
- Introduce relevant spiritual issues.

GROUP COUNSELING

Organizing Group Counseling

- Work with local agencies and universities.
- Use effective publicity.
- Have small gender separate groups.
- Encourage individual counseling as well.
- Establish a safe and comfortable place.
- Document, document, document.
- Remove barriers to participation.
- Develop a format and topics.
- Utilize volunteer activity.
- Budget.

Topics to Include

- Sexuality and body image
- Forgiveness
- Healing
- Suffering and evil
- Anger
- Relationships with family members
- Romantic relationships
- Ways to relieve stress
- Testimonies
- Evaluation

Things Volunteers Can Do

- Facilitate groups.
- Prepare meals and clean up.
- Transport participants.
- Provide a secure presence.
- Provide childcare.
- Donate pillows, stuffed animals, soft balls, etc.

notes

Chapter 1

1. Statistics come from RAINN calculations of 2000 National Crime Victimization Survey, Bureau of Justice Statistics, U.S. Department of Justice; Sex Offenses and Offenders, Bureau of Justice Statistics, U.S. Department of Justice 1997; and Assault of Young Children as Reported to Law Enforcement, Bureau of Justice Statistics, U.S. Department of Justice 2000. See http://www.rainn.org/

Chapter 2

1. According to Carrie Marie Rennison, Bureau of Justice Statistics, U.S. Department of Justice, *National Crime Victimization Survey: Changes 1998–1999 with Trends 1993–1999, at 11 (2000)*, available at http://www.rainn.org/ncvs99.pdf, 28.3 percent of rapes were reported to police in 1999, down from 31.6 percent in 1998. Among all violent crimes, 44 percent of victims reported their attack to police.

Chapter 10

1. Judith Lewis Herman, *Trauma and Recovery: The Aftermath of Violence—From Domestic Abuse to Political Terror* (New York: BasicBooks, 1992), 36.

2. Ibid., 47.

3. Quoted in Robin Warshaw, *I Never Called It Rape: The Ms. Report on Recognizing, Fighting and Surviving Date and Acquaintance Rape* (New York: HarperPerennial, 1988), 68.

4. Ibid., 73.

5. Ibid., 74.

6. *Decisions of the 203rd General Assembly on Human Sexuality: Presbyterians and Human Sexuality 1991* (Louisville: Office of the General Assembly Presbyterian Church (U.S.A.), 1991), 43.

7. Frank S. Frick, *A Journey Through the Hebrew Scriptures* (New York: Harcourt Brace College Publishers, 1995), 446–53.

8. Renita Weems, "Song of Songs," *The Women's Bible Commentary*, ed. Sharon H. Ringe and Carol A. Newson (Louisville: Westminster John Knox Press, 1992), 157.

9. Weems, "Song of Songs," 159–60.

Chapter 11

1. Judith Lewis Herman, *Trauma and Recovery: The Aftermath of Violence—From Domestic Abuse to Political Terror* (New York: BasicBooks, 1992), 178.

2. David Ray Griffin, *God, Power, and Evil: A Process Theodicy* (Philadelphia: Westminster Press, 1976), 9.

3. Kent D. Richmond, *Preaching to Sufferers: God and the Problem of Pain* (Nashville: Abingdon, 1988), 38–39.

4. Richmond, *Preaching to Sufferers*, 52.

5. Herman, *Trauma and Recovery*, 178.

6. Marie M. Fortune, *Sexual Violence: The Unmentionable Sin, An Ethical and Pastoral Perspective* (New York: Pilgrim Press, 1983), 197.

7. Quoted in James Poling, *The Abuse of Power: A Theological Problem* (Nashville: Abingdon, 1991), 47.

8. Richmond, *Preaching to Sufferers*, 69.

9. Wendy Farley, *Tragic Vision and Divine Compassion: A Contemporary Theodicy* (Louisville: Westminster John Knox Press, 1990), 118–19.

Chapter 12

1. Louise Thornton, "Uncle Karl," in *I Never Told Anyone: Writings by Women Survivors of Child Sexual Abuse*, ed. Ellen Bass and Louis Thornton (New York: Harper & Row, 1983), 154.

2. Marie Fortune, "Forgiveness: The Last Step," *Violence against Women and Children: A Christian Theological Sourcebook*, ed. Carol J. Adams and Marie M. Fortune (New York: Continuum, 1995), 202.

3. Ibid., 202.

4. Ibid., 203–4.

5. Marie M. Fortune, *Sexual Violence: The Unmentionable Sin, an Ethical and Pastoral Perspective* (New York: Pilgrim Press, 1983), 210–13.

6. Fortune, "Forgiveness," 203.

7. Ibid., 201.

bibliography

BOOKS THAT INFLUENCED MY THINKING ABOUT THE BODY AND SEXUALITY

Decisions of the 203rd General Assembly on Human Sexuality: Presbyterians and Human Sexuality 1991. Louisville: Office of the General Assembly Presbyterian Church (U.S.A.), 1991.

Frick, Frank S. *A Journey Through the Hebrew Scriptures.* New York: Harcourt Brace College Publishers, 1995.

Gollwitzer, Helmut. *Song of Love: A Biblical Understanding of Sex.* Trans. Keith Crim. Philadelphia: Fortress Press, 1979.

Goulder, Michael D. *The Song of Fourteen Songs.* Journal of the Old Testament Supplement Series. 36. Sheffield, England: JSOT Press, 1986.

Kelly, Liz. *Surviving Sexual Violence.* Minneapolis: University of Minneapolis Press, 1988.

Nelson, James. *Embodiment: An Approach to Sexuality and Christian Theology.* Minneapolis: Augsburg Publishing, 1978.

Nelson, James. *Body Theology.* Louisville: Westminster John Knox Press, 1992.

Trible, Phyllis. *God and the Rhetoric of Sexuality.* Philadelphia: Fortress Press, 1978.

United Methodist Church. *Leader's Guide to Male and Female: Blessed by God.* Nashville: United Methodist Publishing, 1989.

Warshaw, Robin. *I Never Called It Rape: The Ms. Report on Recognizing, Fighting and Surviving Date and Acquaintance Rape.* New York: Harper Perennial, 1988.

Weems, Renita J. "Song of Songs," *The Women's Bible Commentary.* Ed. Sharon H. Ringe and Carol A. Newsom. Louisville: Westminster John Knox Press, 1992.

BOOKS THAT INFLUENCED MY THINKING ABOUT SUFFERING AND EVIL

Beker, J. Christian. *Suffering and Hope: The Biblical Vision and the Human Predicament.* Grand Rapids: William B. Eerdmans, 1987.

Farley, Wendy. *Tragic Vision and Divine Compassion: A Contemporary Theodicy.* Louisville: Westminster John Knox Press, 1990.

Griffin, David Ray. *God, Power and Evil: a Process Theodicy.* Philadelphia: Westminster Press, 1976.

Hartshorne, Charles. *Omnipotence and Other Theological Mistakes.* Albany: SUNY Press, 1984.

Poling, James N. *The Abuse of Power: A Theological Problem.* Nashville: Abingdon, 1991.

Richmond, Kent D. *Preaching to Sufferers: God and the Problem of Pain.* Nashville: Abingdon, 1988.

Wilson-Kastner, Patricia. "Theological Perspectives on Sexual Violence," *Sexual Assault and Abuse: A Handbook for Clergy and Religious Professionals.* Ed. Mary D. Pellauer et. al. San Francisco: Harper, 1987.

BOOKS THAT INFLUENCED MY THINKING ABOUT FORGIVENESS

Bass, Ellen, and Louise Thornton, eds. *I Never Told Anyone: Writings by Women Survivors of Child Sexual Abuse.* New York: Harper & Row, 1983.

Bonhoeffer, Dietrich. *The Cost of Discipleship.* London: SCM Press, 1959.

Brizee, Robert. *Eight Paths to Forgiveness.* St. Louis: Chalice Press, 1998.

Patton, John. *Is Human Forgiveness Possible?: A Pastoral Care Perspective.* Nashville: Abingdon, 1985.

Suchocki, Marjorie Hewitt. *Fall to Violence: Original Sin in Relational Theology.* New York Continuum, 1994.